PROUD

PROUD

LIVING MY AMERICAN DREAM

YOUNG READERS EDITION

IBTIHAJ MUHAMMAD

LITTLE, BROWN AND COMPANY
New York Boston

Little, Brown and Company
Hachette Book Group
1290 Avenue of the Americas, New York, NY 10104
Visit us at LBYR.com

First Edition: July 2018

Little, Brown and Company is a division of Hachette Book Group, Inc.
The Little, Brown name and logo are trademarks of Hachette Book Group, Inc.

The publisher is not responsible for websites (or their content) that are not owned by
the publisher.

ISBNs: 978-0-316-47700-0 (hardcover), 978-0-316-47701-7 (ebook)

Printed in the United States of America

LSC-C

10 9 8 7 6 5 4 3 2 1

*To anyone who has ever been told they
don't belong. When you let your light shine,
it illuminates everyone around you.*

— CONTENTS —

CONTENTS

— PROLOGUE —

"Muhammad...?" the substitute teacher said as she squinted and brought the attendance sheet closer to her face. She was stuck, and I could guess why: She didn't know how to pronounce my first name.

"Is your last name Muhammad?" she asked, her eyes fixed on me, the only fourth grader in the classroom wearing a hijab, which is a head covering worn in public by many women of the Islamic faith.

"Yes," I answered, nodding. My eyes stayed glued to the seat in front of me.

"And how do you pronounce your first name, young lady?" she asked.

"It's Ibtihaj. Ib-tee-haj." I said each syllable as slowly as possible. "It's pronounced just like it's written." That usually helped people understand how to say it, but not Ms. Winter. She made another face, the kind you make when you taste something bitter.

"Oh, that's too hard," she responded, shaking her head. "We're going to call you Ibti."

"Okay," I agreed, but the way she said "Ibti" made my cheeks burn. I refused to look around to see if my classmates were laughing at me, or worse, pitying me for having a name that was too hard to pronounce.

During recess I did some quick calculating in my head. My friend Jennifer had eight letters in her name, and Elizabeth Brewster had nine in hers. Yet their names weren't "too hard." They weren't assigned nicknames. Why was I? "Ibtihaj" was easy. All my friends could say it, and we were nine! Ms. Winter hadn't even *tried*.

The truth is, for as far back as I can remember, my name has been too difficult or different for some people. The way I identify myself has been even more confusing to them: Black but Muslim. Muslim but American. A hijab-wearing athlete. I've walked into many rooms and stood on stages where it was clear people didn't know what to make of me.

And that's why I wrote *Proud*. I want people to understand who *I* really am, and to get to know the journey behind such headlines as FIRST MUSLIM WOMAN TO COMPETE IN THE OLYMPIC GAMES REPRESENTING THE UNITED STATES. I wrote this book because I wanted to chronicle my quest to challenge society's limited perceptions of what a Muslim woman, a black woman, or an athlete can be.

I want people to know that much of my strength as an athlete comes from how hard I had to work to defy stereotypes, and how I had to show up to the party even when I hadn't been invited. Along the way I learned how to be tough and determined. I had to expect more of myself because no one else did, and I had to have the guts to pursue what I wanted even though it meant charting my own path. I didn't have any role models who looked like me in fencing, and there weren't any other Muslim women wearing hijab at the elite levels of sport to inspire my quest. I had myself, my family, and my faith, and that was enough for me to persist.

I come after many who traveled this path before me: Jackie Robinson, Muhammad Ali, Althea Gibson, John Carlos, Mahmoud Abdul-Rauf, Serena and Venus Williams. These are people who overcame others' doubt and triumphed. Who had barriers put up in front of them and doors slammed in their faces. If you've had an opportunity taken from you because of your race, religion, or gender, I hope *Proud* inspires you. I hope you can feel empowered by my fight and know that—with hard work, patience, and determination—you can make your dreams come true.

This book is a memoir, not an autobiography. The stories and opinions are based upon my memories and are true as I remember them. Some names and identifying details have been changed, and some characters are combinations of people who've passed through my life. In order to keep things moving forward, I've also compressed time in some instances. But for the most part, this book is a true recollection of the story of my life.

And what a story it's been! If someone had told me that my life would unfold the way it has—full of untold blessings and endless opportunities—because I picked up a sword at thirteen years old, I would not have believed them. But I did pick up that sword, and despite the uphill battle, it has been a rewarding journey. It's my hope that you find your own sword to use in a way that brings you happiness and success, and that the word "no" becomes your motivation to press forward. Inshallah, so may it be.

1

Growing Up

In search of my mother's garden, I found my own.

—Alice Walker

"Can't you ask your dad? Maybe he'll say yes this time," my best friend, Amy, asked as we sat in her backyard. She wanted me to come to her sleepover birthday party, but I knew the chances were slim to none. The rules were pretty clear in our house: no sleepovers. But I *really* wanted to go! All the girls at school were having slumber parties now, and I was convinced I was the only kid at Seth Boyden Elementary School who wasn't allowed to attend them.

"You know my dad," I said, sighing, "but I'll ask him anyway."

"Just try to butter him up," Amy suggested. "Give him a hug."

I smiled. Abu loved my hugs.

I knew I'd find my dad in his room getting ready to go to his evening shift at the precinct. He'd gotten promoted to detective, so he didn't have to wear his regular police uniform like he used to. But he was still a cop through and through, and he had the same strict expectations at home that he had at work. His children knew not to question his authority or bend the rules. But I still held out hope that I'd change Abu's mind, because I *really* wanted to go to Amy's birthday party.

I knocked on the door. "Abu," I called out quietly, using the Arabic word for "father." "Can I come in?"

I found Abu sitting on the bed, pulling on his socks. He was a big man, with such a serious way about him that I could understand why some people found him intimidating. But I didn't. I loved everything about him, from his full, scratchy beard to the way he was willing to sacrifice anything for our family. I put a big smile on my face and, remembering Amy's advice, walked over to him, sat on the bed, and enveloped him in a hug.

"Abu," I said, pulling away to look into his big brown eyes. "My best friend, Amy, across the street, is having a sleepover party for her birthday and wants to know if I can go. Can I?"

Abu didn't even pause before answering. "Ibtihaj, you know the rules. No sleepovers. You won't be sleeping at anyone's house except this one. It's not safe."

"But you let me sleep at Auntie and Uncle Bernard's house!"

"That's different. They're family," he insisted, standing up and walking past me toward the door.

I followed him down the carpeted steps to the living room. My mom was there putting my little sister Faizah to sleep on her lap. She still had on her hijab and what she called her "teaching clothes": dark, long, wide-legged pants and a cotton tunic top. As a special-education teacher, Mom often found herself having to get on the floor with her students.

"What's going on?" Mom asked, noting the frustrated look on my face.

"Amy wants me to sleep over at her house for her birthday, but Abu said no," I whimpered. Then I stared at her with puppy-dog eyes, hoping she could make my dad change his mind.

She glanced up at Abu and took in what was going on

3

between us. He wasn't going to change his mind. Even *I* could tell that.

"You know the rules, Ibtihaj," my mother said sweetly, trying to make the bad news sound better. One of the key teachings of Islam is that we should always respect our parents, so I wasn't going to put up a fight. But I was still *so* disappointed. Sometimes Mommy could help make Abu see things differently, like the time she convinced him to let us keep a stray cat that we had found in the garage even though Abu claimed he didn't like pets. The cat ran away after only a few days, but because Abu had seen how well we took care of it, he surprised us and brought home a beautiful umbrella cockatoo that he'd found wandering the streets while he was on duty. Now Koocah was a real member of our family.

"Abu, the kids who are coming to the party are just the girls from my class," I said. "There won't be any boys there." According to our faith, I wasn't allowed to hang out with boys socially, so I hoped that maybe, just maybe, this might convince Abu.

My father was collecting his keys, wallet, and glasses like he did every time he was leaving the house. He stopped moving and turned to face me. "Ibtihaj, no sleepovers means no sleepovers." The firmness of his voice told me that the discussion was over.

He walked over to me as I began to tear up. His tone was loving as he pulled me close. "Ibtihaj, you don't need to cry about this. It's going to be okay." He smoothed down the stray hairs that had escaped from my braids.

But I couldn't stop crying. We had a lot of rules in our house. We couldn't watch television during the week, we couldn't listen to music on the radio, we had to wear our hijabs to school twice a week, and we prayed five times a day. Some of the rules came from the Quran—the ancient, sacred book followed by Muslims—but some, like the sleepover rule, were because Abu was protective.

I know now that Abu was strict because he loved us so much. He was a cop and saw bad things happen to good people every day. He also didn't want any of his kids to end up where he and Mommy had come from.

Both of my parents were born and raised in Newark, New Jersey. In 1967, when they were teens, the Newark riots broke out. Newark's black residents were protesting the city's racism and frequent incidents of police brutality. The riots went on for five days straight, and when they were over, 26 people were dead, 750 were injured, and over 1,000 people had been arrested. Most of the victims were black. In the aftermath most business owners on Springfield Avenue, Newark's commercial strip, didn't rebuild and left their stores abandoned and boarded up. Most of the white people who could afford to fled the city, and soon Newark became known for its empty houses, unemployment, and poverty. Drug dealers and criminals lived on practically every block.

My mother, Denise, watched the riots, and though they frightened her, they didn't feel totally unexpected. Violence had always been part of her neighborhood. But she had a plan to break free. Like her sister, Diana, who was eleven years older, had a good job, and lived in New York City, my mom knew she had to do well in school and stay off the streets.

My mom said her friends and relatives always made fun of her because she refused to hang out with them on the weekends. They said she was too serious and needed to learn how to have some fun. But my mother was afraid of what would happen if she partied, even for a night. She didn't want to end up like so many of her neighbors: poor, in jail, or unemployed and hopeless. So my mother stayed home as much as she could, and when she felt like she had to get out, she'd walk just a few blocks to visit her cousin Sharon.

Sharon came from Mommy's mother's side of the family and was only a few years older than my mom, but she had the kind of home my mother didn't. Sharon didn't have violent fights with her husband, Karim, and their small apartment felt like an oasis from the chaos in the streets. In fact, it was one of the only places my mother felt safe. Karim worked as a mechanic, and he was always home by 6:00 PM, so Sharon never paced the living room wondering where he was.

Sharon was like a big sister to my mom, and their conversations flowed easily. One night, while watching Sharon prepare dinner, my mom asked her cousin a personal question. "Sharon, how did you find a guy like Karim, who's not all caught up in the streets?"

"Girl, Karim is a Muslim," Sharon said. "You have to find yourself a Muslim man to marry. They will always do right by you."

"Karim's a Muslim?" my mom asked. "Like he's part of the Nation?" She knew that the Nation of Islam was a movement whose goal was to improve African Americans' lives and place in society, but it had also been criticized for embracing violence.

"No, Karim says the Nation is more interested in starting a revolution than getting right with God."

"Are you going to become a Muslim?" Mom asked.

Sharon shrugged. "I'm thinking about it. Karim wants me to, especially before we have children."

My mom thought about how Karim respected and loved Sharon, which was so unlike the way her own father treated her mother.

"Girl," she said with a sigh, "I'd convert in a second if it meant my husband was going to treat me as well as Karim treats you."

It was at that moment that the thought of converting to Islam was planted in my mother's brain. My mom started to study the Muslim men and women around the neighborhood. The men who belonged to the Nation were easy to recognize because they wore bow ties and stood in front of the storefront mosques where they went to worship. The women wore long dresses and head coverings. They all seemed so sure of themselves, so proud. My mom started to visit Sharon more often, since she and Karim were the only people Mommy could talk to about Islam. They kept an English-language version of the Quran on their coffee table, and my mom liked to flip through the pages, searching for a message that would confirm that she was on the right path.

The simple, poetic writing captivated my mother's spirit. She fell in love with Islam and the peaceful guidance that it offered. She started thinking about God as Allah, who was the one god of Islam. My mom put her short skirts away and decided to dress modestly, as the Quran instructed. She liked the idea that by wearing long pants and long skirts, she was in control of how others saw her body. By the time my mom started college at Rutgers University, she knew Islam was allowing her to reinvent her life. Islam gave her more to believe in than what was in front of her.

Unlike my mother, my father, Eugene, discovered Islam from his siblings. He was one of the youngest of twelve children, and all his older brothers had joined the Nation of Islam before my father hit his teen years. The Nation of Islam appealed to many black men in Newark because it offered spiritual guidance in the midst of all the city's chaos, and its message uplifted black men in a nation that discriminated against them.

Abu's parents separated when Abu was only five, so he was attracted to Islam's emphasis on the family and the important role of the father. Along with a group of friends, Abu founded a new mosque in East Orange, New Jersey. It was there that he first saw my mother, who had come to my father's mosque to officially take her *shahaadah*, or declaration of faith. She seemed to love the religion and was dedicated to learning everything she could in the class for new converts. My father was immediately attracted to her, and sometimes he would peek into the classroom where she was reading verses from the Quran, her glasses sliding down her nose.

My father asked some of his friends to find out all they could about my mom, and he soon learned that her name was Denise but she had chosen the name Inayah when she converted. Following Muslim tradition, members of the mosque formally introduced my parents, and they went on a handful of dates to see if they made a good match. They did. My mother liked my father's quiet sense of humor and his ambition—in addition to running the mosque, he also owned two small restaurants in Newark. My father fell in love with my mother's beauty, her enthusiasm for life, and her love of children. She was a nurturer and immediately made my father feel comfortable in his own skin. My father didn't hesitate to make his intentions known, first to my mother's parents and then to her. They were married a short time later, first signing their Islamic marriage contract in a traditional ceremony, called *nikah*, and then later holding a more formal celebration.

As part of their new life, my parents went by the names Inayah and Shamsiddin. Their chosen names symbolized their dedication to Allah, which extended to all aspects of their lives. They wanted a big family, and that's what they got. First came Brandilyn; then a son, Qareeb, five years later; then me less than two years after that; and within six more years, two girls named Asiya and Faizah. My parents had agreed to raise their children following

Muslim traditions, so all meals would be halal, or prepared according to Muslim dietary laws, and we prayed five times a day. Hijab—which was prescribed in the Quran but was still a personal choice—would be observed for their daughters, meaning we would cover our heads when we reached our teens. No matter what, family and faith would always come first, and they did. Our home was always full of love and joy—for one another and for Allah.

My mother vowed her children would never end up victims of the streets. My father vowed we would always have a father in our lives. And so they found a spacious second-floor apartment in a quiet residential section of Newark and a private Islamic academy for us to attend. Even though it was a struggle to send their children to a private school, both of my parents were willing to sacrifice for our spiritual education. Always wanting to help his community, Abu became a police officer when I was three. He secured good insurance for us, and he and my mom saved their money. In just a few years they had enough to buy a cozy four-bedroom home in Maplewood, New Jersey.

The picturesque suburban township of Maplewood felt about as far away from Newark as you can imagine. I was five when we drove into town, passing block after block of perfect brick homes with tidy lawns and manicured gardens. When Abu stopped in front of our new house, the first thing I noticed was the green front door, which looked warm and welcoming. The house was three stories and painted white, with mint-colored shutters on the second-story windows. Everything was compact, including the small, square front yard, which didn't look big enough for a good game of tag. Then Abu told Brandilyn, Qareeb, me, and little Asiya to get out of the car. His eyes twinkled as he said, "I want to show you something special."

The four of us followed my dad down the long driveway to the back of the house. There in front of us was a huge in-ground swimming pool.

I wanted to jump in the water right then and there.

"Can we go swimming, Abu?" I begged.

"Ibtihaj, you don't know how to swim," my father said with a laugh.

"I know, but I can do a cannonball. Can't I, Qareeb?"

"I don't want any one of you kids even near this pool without me or your mother next to you," my father said sternly. "But I'm going to teach you all how to swim. That's why we bought this house."

I didn't know anyone who had a swimming pool in their backyard. In fact, most of my friends lived in apartments, like we always had, so no one even *had* a backyard. And if we wanted to play outside, our moms usually took

12

us to the park, but even then they were always worried, telling us to keep our eyes open and pay attention to our surroundings. But this house, with grass and a backyard and plenty of room to play, was totally different. It was full of promise for a happier, more carefree life.

This promise extended to the town, too. Everything about Maplewood seemed different from Newark. Newark was gritty, with a lot of pavement and worn-down buildings. Maplewood was pure, full of trees and parks. The downtown area looked like something out of an old movie, with restaurants, cafés, bakeries, and bookstores. The park in the center of town even had a duck pond and white wooden gazebos.

My parents knew they had made the right decision to raise their family in Maplewood. In addition to the fact that it was so family friendly, with good public schools, libraries, and a community center, it was also racially and economically diverse. When we arrived there in the early '90s, the city was approximately 59 percent white and 33 percent black. Though there was only one other Muslim family in town, and the women didn't wear hijab like we did, I still found friends and felt at home right away. My first and best friend was Amy.

Amy had big, round brown eyes and long black hair, which she always wore in two lopsided ponytails.

I remember soon after we moved in, Amy crossed the street with her mother and came to say hello. Then while our mothers talked, Amy asked me if I had a bicycle.

"Yeah, I have a bicycle," I said. "It's purple and pink. Pink's my favorite color."

"My bike's pink, too!" Amy said with a big smile on her face. "I can't wait to show you!"

After that, it didn't take Amy and me long to set up a routine for playing. First, we'd grab our bikes and ride up and down our driveway, talking about all the things we were going to do when school started in the fall, and when we grew bored of that, we'd head over to her backyard and play until our moms called us in for dinner.

Not long after we moved in, Amy asked me a question. "Ibtihaj, how come your mom always wears a scarf on her head?"

No one had ever asked me that before. All my friends in Newark had moms who wore hijab. In fact, I didn't have any friends, except Amy, who had a mother who let her hair out in public.

I had to stop and think for a minute before I could answer Amy's question. "My mom wears hijab because we're Muslim," I said.

"What's a Muslim?" Amy asked, a frown wrinkling her suntanned face.

I looked at my new friend and wondered why she didn't know what it meant to be Muslim. "It's our religion."

"When you grow up, are you going to wear the same thing on your head like your mom does?" Amy asked.

I shrugged. "Yeah, I guess so. Sometimes I wear a scarf now for special occasions."

"That's cool," Amy said, obviously satisfied with my answers. "You wanna go over to your house?"

"Yeah, let's go," I said, jumping up and wiping the grass from my legs. Then I looked over at Amy and smiled. Even then I realized how lucky I was to have a friend who didn't care that I was different.

I plopped down on the floor of the bedroom I shared with my sister Asiya. Asiya was only five, but she was a good listener. My mom always joked that was because I talked so much.

"What's the matter?" Asiya asked me as I picked up a Barbie doll from our stash. I *loved* playing with Barbies.

"I hope Mommy can convince Abu to let me go to Amy's birthday party," I said to Asiya. "Amy really wants me to be there. And I should be there because we're best friends."

"But we never sleep over anywhere," Asiya said.

I shook my head at my sister. What did she know? I turned back to my Barbie, and a short time later I heard my mother calling me.

"Ibtihaj, come here, please."

Asiya looked at me, and I smiled. I hoped my mother had good news for me. I ran down the stairs and saw her waiting for me, still seated on the couch. My baby sister, Faizah, was asleep in a rocking seat near her.

"Where's Abu?" I asked.

"He left for work," my mom said. She patted the seat cushion next to her, and I leaped over to the couch and snuggled up to my mom. I loved Faizah, but she took up a lot of my mother's time, so when I got the chance, I liked to be as close to Mommy as possible. She was warm and soft, and she smelled like comfort. I loved that we looked the most alike, with our matching golden skin and hazel-colored eyes.

My mother turned and lifted my head toward her. "Ibtihaj, you know your father and I make rules to keep you and your siblings safe. It's not safe for you to sleep over at other people's homes when we don't know who's going to be there."

"But it's Amy's house. You know them," I said, trying not to whine.

"I know," my mom answered, "but rules are rules."

I hung my head in defeat. Amy was going to be

disappointed, and once again I would be the odd one out on Monday when everyone was talking about the latest slumber party.

"But..." My mother wasn't done. "I convinced your father that since we *do* know Amy and her family, and since they *do* live right across the street, you can go to the birthday party."

"Yes!" I shouted, jumping off the couch.

My mother shushed me, pointing to the sleeping baby. "Don't get too excited. I said you can go, but we will pick you up around eight thirty, so no sleeping over."

To me this was still a win. I just wanted to be there so I'd have fun stories to tell on Monday, too.

"Thank you, Mommy," I squealed, gave her a big hug, and dashed out the door.

Amy's party was fun. Most of the girls from our third-grade class were there, and we played in Amy's backyard until the sun set. Then Amy's mom called us all in for pizza and soda, telling us we could eat as much as we wanted. After that, Amy's mother brought in a big sheet cake decorated with pink and yellow flowers, and we all sang "Happy Birthday" and watched Amy open her presents. By the time my mom came to pick me up, the rest of the girls were changing into their pajamas and brushing their teeth because bedtime was in one hour.

Some of the other girls were sad or confused by the fact that I was leaving—and a tiny part of me was, too—but it was okay. I'd rather be with my family. Plus, the only thing about the sleepover I was going to miss was the sleeping part!

— CHAPTER —
2

Work for the Win

Just try new things. Don't be afraid. Step out of your
comfort zones and soar.

—Michelle Obama

My brother, Qareeb, was eighteen months older than
me—and one year ahead of me in school—and he made
my childhood a big adventure. He was the person I most
wanted to be like, and I made it my mission to keep up
with him, even if I knew it would land us in trouble
and me sometimes in tears. Whether he was daring me
to jump off the top bunk of our bunk beds or racing me
down the block, I was always one step behind him, trying my best to keep up. I had the quiet determination
of my mother, and Qareeb had the boisterous nature of

Abu and his brothers, but we were best friends. Our older sister, Brandilyn, knew to stay away from Qareeb's rambunctious energy, Asiya was too small to keep up with us, and Faizah was just a baby, so for a while it was me and Qareeb against the world.

"Can we do it one more time?" I asked Abu one night during a pool race. I had finished just behind Qareeb that last time, and I knew I could finally beat him if I had one more chance.

"I don't wanna race again," Qareeb whined. "I'm tired."

"What? You're scared I'll beat you this time?" I said, knowing Qareeb could never turn down a challenge.

Abu was laughing from his lawn chair by the side of the pool. "Let's see if you'll let your little sister beat you, Qareeb," he teased. Qareeb dog-paddled over next to me, and we both stood waiting for Abu's signal. I fixed my gaze on the opposite end of the pool and put my foot against the pool's wall. Abu yelled, "Go!"

I moved my arms as fast as I could, cutting through the water. My legs were like motors, up and down, up and down; I moved just like Abu had taught me. My head was down, so I couldn't see where my brother was, and I didn't stop to find out. When I slammed my hand on the edge of the pool at the deep end, I heard Abu screaming in triumph, and I knew I had done it.

I paddled over to the ladder, hauled myself out of the pool, and leaped into my father's open arms. "Ibtihaj, you did just what I taught you," he said proudly. "You kept your head down and used those long legs of yours."

I was ecstatic and spun my head to look for Qareeb. He was sitting at the edge of the pool looking angry. Abu waved at him to come join us anyway. "You're going to have to work harder to beat Ibtihaj now, boy. She's tasted victory."

Both my parents thought of sports almost as a way of life. Abu believed that they'd give us a competitive edge, making us winners on the field and in life. He taught all of us how to swim, play baseball, basketball, and any other sport he could get us involved in. And he had us competing against one another as often as possible.

Mommy liked athletics because they kept us active and engaged with kids from school and around the neighborhood. Both she and Abu believed that sports were the best way to keep all of us kids disciplined, out of trouble, and continuing to learn outside of the classroom. That's why I can't remember a single time in my life when we weren't expected to play something.

"Get the rec book, Ibtihaj," my mother yelled from the kitchen. "You're next." It was a Saturday in early spring, and the new Maplewood Recreation booklet had just arrived in our mailbox. That meant it was time for all the kids to pick a sports program for the summer. Qareeb was twelve, and he was probably going to select baseball or basketball. He was also a part of the local youth track team, the Jaguars, and played football in the fall. Asiya, now seven, decided to try gymnastics.

I grabbed the booklet and walked into the kitchen. I plopped down at the table while my mother started making lunch. We had just moved Koocah's cage from the living room to the kitchen, where we spent most of our time. As Koocah stretched her wings and soaked up the afternoon sun pouring in from the skylight, I flipped through the pages. There were so many different programs to choose from. I had already tried T-ball and tennis. Both soccer and lacrosse were big sports in our town, but they didn't really interest me.

I pushed the booklet away with a sigh.

"What's the matter? You can't find anything that you like?" my mother asked.

"Nope," I said. "Can't I just swim and work in my

garden this summer?" I had a small garden out back near the pool that Mommy had helped me plant. I had plans to try growing eggplants along with my tomatoes.

I knew I had to pick a program, though, because Mommy taught summer school, and she couldn't just leave five kids at home alone all day. So she signed us up for the summer program at the Roseville Avenue mosque in Newark, which was a few blocks over from her school. Afterward she would drop us off at practice.

"What about track?" she asked. "You could join the Jaguars with Qareeb."

I started to get nervous. Even though Qareeb really seemed to enjoy running track, and the kids on the team seemed nice, I wasn't sure if I was fast enough. I also worried I'd suffer in the summer heat. "I don't know, Mommy," I said. "It's going to be really hot."

"Oh, you'll be fine," she said. "We'll pack you a water bottle."

"Um, I don't know," I tried again, then added, "Mommy, what would I wear?" I didn't know how, as a young Muslim girl, I could wear the team uniform, which consisted of a tank top and shorts.

My mom waved away that thought. "We'll find you some leggings and a T-shirt to run in. Don't worry."

I wanted to point out that running in leggings would

make the heat even more unbearable, but I kept that thought to myself. Instead I asked, "What if I don't like it?"

"What if you don't like what? The uniform?"

"What if I don't like track?" I said again. "You know running isn't really my thing."

"You could have fooled me with the amount of time you and Qareeb spend running around this house," my mother huffed. "You might as well use all that energy at track practice, where it belongs."

"I guess I could try it," I said, intentionally showing little enthusiasm.

"Good," my mom said. "I like the coaches over there. They're all black and great role models for both you and Qareeb. I'm sure you'll make some good friends."

I didn't share my mother's excitement, but I knew I didn't really have a choice. A summer without a sport was not in the cards for me.

Because I was only ten and hadn't hit puberty, I wasn't wearing hijab yet. That meant I didn't have to cover my head during practice, which would've been unbearable in the humidity, especially with the spandex leggings I wore to cover my legs. The summer heat was so bad that I was allowed to wear T-shirts, but that was only a small comfort from the relentless sun.

I knew I didn't want to run the long-distance events, and I wasn't sure I was fast enough for the sprints, so I volunteered to run the 800 meter because it was a middle distance—not too fast and not too slow. I showed up at every practice and worked hard, and soon I was surprised to discover that I didn't just like running, I was also pretty good at it! I especially loved the days when we had meets. Once I finished competing in my events, I would huddle in the bleachers with my friends or stand near the concession stand eating warm pretzels and nachos. And the competitive part of me liked the feeling of winning, crossing the finish line and coming home with a medal.

In the middle of July we had our first away meet in northern New Jersey. The coaches told us the meet was really important and that we should get plenty of rest and drink water the night before. The weatherman had forecast record highs, so I knew I was going to be extra hot in my spandex. I also realized someone was going to ask me why I covered my legs. I was going to hate that whole part of the experience, even if I came home with a million medals.

The night before the meet Abu pulled me aside.

"Ibtihaj," he started, "it's going to be really hot

tomorrow, and running in the heat can be dangerous. If you feel faint or like you can't breathe, it's okay to stop."

"Okay, Abu," I said, and wrapped my arms around him. Abu and I tended to bond the most when it came to sports, so when he offered this extra bit of advice, I soaked it up.

The drive to the track meet was two hours, and when we got there, my mom told me and Qareeb to go find our coaches while she woke my sisters up. We both gave her a quick hug and then ran off to find our teammates. I had already worked up a sweat. It felt like one hundred degrees, even though it was actually eighty-five. When it was my turn to race, I prayed that I'd survive the heat. But when the gun went off, I sprang out of the blocks, took the lead, and felt good. I pumped my arms and lengthened my stride. The first two hundred done. But the sun was so strong I could feel its rays on every inch of my body during the second and third laps. I only had to make it around the track one more time, but my legs had started to feel like they were made of lead. Two girls passed me, and then another. I tried to sprint to regain my lead, but I couldn't make my legs go any faster, and my breath started to come in jagged heaves. Suddenly my father's voice popped into my head. "If it hurts to breathe, you can stop." I tried to pull in a breath, but there was a growing pressure. So I slowed down, fell into a trot, and then just started to walk. It was no use. Instead of heading to the finish line, I scanned the bleachers, found my mother and my two sisters, and slowly made my way off the track and over to them.

My mom did not look happy.

"What are you doing?" she yelled before I'd even made it up to their seats.

"Abu said if I couldn't breathe, I could stop," I responded, surprised by her tone.

"No, no, no," she said. "You can't do that!"

"Mommy, but I couldn't breathe!"

"Look, the sun is strong, but you *cannot* stop in the middle of the race," she insisted. "I don't expect you to always win, but I expect you to give one hundred percent."

"But Abu said that if I had trouble breathing…"

Then Qareeb came over, looking confused. "Why'd you stop running, Ibtihaj? You were winning!"

I was now embarrassed and realized that I'd made a big mistake. I looked over at my teammates with tears in my eyes. The other girls had finished, but I hadn't.

I turned back to my mom, feeling terrible. "I'm sorry."

Mom wasn't usually as strict as my dad, but she knew

how to be firm—especially when she wanted to teach me a lesson. She reached toward me and put her hand on my leg, patting it lightly. "Sorry isn't ever going to win the race, Ibtihaj," she said. "You have to work for the win, even if it hurts."

It was then that I realized that winning wasn't going to come easily, and I never wanted to let my mother down. I never wanted to give her a reason to think that I was wasting her time or money, or that I didn't know how to work hard. I promised myself and my mom that next time I would do better. It became my mantra as an athlete.

— CHAPTER —
3

Not the Sport for Me

My mission in life is not merely to survive, but to thrive.

—Maya Angelou

"Why are you wearing that tablecloth on your head?" Jack Bowman, the middle school bully, sneered.

I gritted my teeth and held back the tears that were pressing against my eyelids.

Now that I was wearing hijab to school every.day, my life had gotten complicated. Middle school is typically about fitting in, and that's all I wanted to do. On the one hand, I was a good student, I had a few close friends, and most of my teachers loved me, but it was impossible for me ever to blend in with the crowd. Because of my hijab, I'd never be like everyone else.

My hijab was part of me, though. I didn't see why it

made me any different from the other kids. So what, I wore a scarf to cover my hair. Why was that such a big deal? Other people projected that difference on me. My hijab was also a sign of my maturity and faithfulness to Allah, but I didn't need anyone at Maplewood Middle School to acknowledge that. I just wanted my hijab to be a nonissue.

One of the biggest problems Muslims in America face is that they often are misunderstood. People don't know that Islam is one of the three Abrahamic faiths, Christianity and Judaism being the other two. They don't know that Muslims recognize Moses, Abraham, and Jesus as prophets, though we follow the teachings of the prophet Muhammad. We worship the same god as Christians and Jews do; we simply refer to God as Allah. Many people assume Islam is a foreign religion associated with radicals. The truth is, if people understood the five pillars we live by—believe in one god, pray five times a day, give to the poor, make a pilgrimage to Mecca (the Islamic holy city in Saudi Arabia), and fast during Ramadan (our most sacred month)—they'd probably rethink their attitudes. Sure, we do things a little differently from some people, but I never understood why that was justification for others to be cruel.

There was this one kid, Mike Jackson. For some

reason, Mike wouldn't accept that I had the same rights to attend Maplewood Middle School as he did. He teased me whenever possible. My friends told me to ignore him, which I tried to do, but it was hard because I never knew where or when he'd show up.

One day in seventh grade I was in art class, and we were working with oil paints. I was excited to get started because I *loved* painting. I was concentrating hard, blending the paints to get the colors I wanted, so I didn't notice the shadow creeping up behind me. Suddenly I was blinded by a huge pain in my left arm.

"Ow!" I cried out. Mike Jackson was standing next to me with a smirk on his face.

"Sorry," Mike said, but he obviously didn't mean it. He'd taken advantage of the fact that Ms. Murphy had stepped out into the hall, and had punched me as hard as he could in front of everyone. I could barely see straight from the pain and the humiliation.

"I'm going to tell my brother you hit me," I said, fuming.

Mike shrugged and walked away. I tried my best to focus on my painting, but all I could see was red. I held my face down so no one could witness the hot, angry tears running down my cheeks. Then I wiped my face with my shirtsleeve and tried to pull myself together. *Deep breath,*

Ibtihaj, I told myself, remembering what my mom had said to me the day in third grade when Delia Sanders and her brother, Justin, threw snowballs at me after school. She made me take a deep breath and reminded me that Allah rewards the kind. "So, let it go," she'd said.

As soon as the last bell rang, I found my brother.

"What's up?" he asked when he saw me.

"I need your help," I said, pulling him away from his group of friends.

I told Qareeb about Mike hitting me in the arm. "I said that I'd tell you what he did, but he didn't care. You have to talk to him. He can't do this again."

Qareeb looked angry. "Which one is he?" he asked, already looking around the back lawn of the school, where all the students were dismissed. "He's not going to get away with this." I was so grateful I had a brother who wasn't afraid to stick up for me.

I scanned the crowd of students pouring out of the middle school building and quickly spotted Mike. "That's him," I said, "the ugly one with the red shirt."

My brother gave me a look of surprise. Mike wasn't a very big or scary-looking guy. "Are you sure he punched you on purpose?"

"Yeah, I'm sure," I said with confidence. "He teases me all the time."

"All right, come on." He started pushing through the crowd toward where Mike was standing with a bunch of his friends.

"Yo, Mike, why'd you punch my sister?" Qareeb said, balling his hands into fists and puffing up his chest and shoulders. He almost looked like he'd forgotten to take off his football padding.

"I didn't punch her hard," Mike said, flustered. "I was just playing around and—"

Before Mike could finish his sentence, *KA-POW!* Qareeb punched him in the arm.

"Don't you ever touch my sister again," Qareeb said with extra grit in his voice.

I don't know if it was the pain, the embarrassment of being punched by an eighth grader in front of his friends, or a combination of the two, but Mike started crying. Watching him in tears didn't make me feel as good as I thought it would, but Mike never bothered me again.

Unfortunately, there were always others to take his place.

"Mommy, do I have to wear my hijab today?" I asked early one morning.

My mother stopped what she was doing and gave me a look that could have been pity, shame, or disappointment.

"Yes, you have to wear it." My mother sighed. "It might be hard at times, but remember, this is all part of Allah's plan. I promise you as you get older, you'll understand that wearing hijab is a gift, not a punishment."

She was right, and I did eventually come to see hijab as a gift. But my seventh-grade self, who just wanted to feel like everyone else and avoid bullying, wasn't fully convinced. Still, I put on my hijab that day and never again asked if I could leave it at home. I tolerated the teasing and tried to keep my attention on the things I loved about school. It wasn't always easy, but I would tell myself that if I got good grades and was the smartest in the class, I could be happy enough.

Like any bullied kid, though, sometimes I would fantasize about the future, when I would be successful and famous. I would come back to Maplewood and find all the people who had made my life difficult, and I would say to them, "See, you thought you could break me, but you didn't!"

My mom and dad were the other reason I tried to do well in school. Like many parents, especially those in the Muslim community, my parents demanded academic excellence from their children. If we didn't bring home all

As on our report cards, they punished us. My parents also had high expectations for our professional future. They expected us to choose one of two prestigious careers: doctor or lawyer.

As soon I turned eleven, my mother enrolled me in summer precollege programs at places like the New Jersey Institute of Technology (NJIT) and the University of Medicine and Dentistry of New Jersey. These courses were specifically targeted to high-achieving black and Latino children, and I loved that the teachers there praised me for being smart and hardworking. As a bonus, everyone else looked like me: brown. Even the teachers. There weren't any other Muslim students, but the sense of inclusion there still made me feel like I could be myself and never worry about an ignorant person saying something mean to me.

The philosophy behind these selective summer programs was to get minority children on a college-prep track as soon as possible. Not only did we have advanced academic classes, we were also taught time-management skills, essay writing, and public speaking. The teachers showed us college applications and how to apply for financial aid. They didn't promise us anything, but they told us if we worked hard and took advantage of every opportunity presented to us, we would succeed.

The first summer I attended the program, I met a girl named Damaris, who lived in South Orange, a neighboring town to Maplewood. Damaris's mother was black and her father was Filipino. She had golden-honey skin, almost the same color as mine, and a nice smile. Despite her biracial background, Damaris strongly identified as black. She was always quoting famous black writers and activists. We had almost every class together that summer, and we became close friends in a short amount of time. She didn't care that I was a Muslim and didn't need me to teach her all about my religion, because she had a cousin who was Muslim.

I didn't have any friends at school who were so similar to me. Damaris was the kind of friend I desperately wanted so I wouldn't feel so alone sometimes—like when I scanned my class and didn't see any black faces, or when someone asked me why my mom wore "that thing on her head." Sure, my childhood best friend, Amy, had always accepted me, but when we reached middle school we'd had different teachers and few classes in common, so we'd drifted apart. I needed friends like Damaris who just *got* me.

"I wish you could transfer to my school for eighth grade," I told Damaris on the phone one night.

"Yeah, that would be great," she said. "But at least we'll be in high school together for four years." Damaris always looked on the bright side. "And when we are, you can also meet my friends Stacey and Ana."

If Damaris's friends were anything like her, I knew I'd like them. I still had one more year at Maplewood Middle School, and I wasn't looking forward to dealing with the people who made my days difficult. Sometimes I wished I could skip the last year of middle school.

"You can make it, Ibtihaj," Damaris said when I told her about some of the bullying I'd faced. "You're stronger than you think, and you're crazy smart. My mom always says, 'Our ancestors fought too hard for us to give up now.'"

I smiled. "Thanks, Damaris. You're the best."

"I know," she said, laughing. "And don't you forget it."

Even though I didn't tell my mother about every single time someone was mean to me at school, she wasn't unaware of my feelings of isolation. She knew how badly I wanted to fit in with my classmates and the girls on the school softball team. And she had witnessed some of the cattiness at the mosque that I had to deal with, too. Because I attended public school instead of a private Islamic academy, a lot of the girls my age at the masjid (another name for "mosque") wouldn't talk to me. They claimed anyone who went to public school was probably going to become trouble.

My mother rolled her eyes whenever she heard about "that nonsense," as she called it. "Those girls don't know what they're talking about, and their parents should be ashamed of themselves for letting them think that way," she said. "Just ignore them and focus on school."

At the end of the day, I had to put my trust in my parents and believe them when they said that if I just worked hard, then everything would solve itself. That trust helped me survive my first years in hijab and middle school.

But I still searched for something to help me fit in.

One day during the fall of my eighth-grade year, my mom and I went to pick up Qareeb from school. He was a freshman now at Columbia High, the same school I'd be attending the following year. As we pulled up to the front of the school, my mom poked me on the arm and pointed toward some windows. "What do you think they're doing in there?" she said, craning her neck to get a better view of what looked like a bunch of students sword fighting in the school cafeteria.

I rolled my window down to look, but all I could see were kids wearing white pants, white jackets, and what looked like masks, dancing around with long, thin swords.

"I have no idea," I said, uninterested in whatever was taking place in there. Instead I was scanning the high school girls pouring out of the massive building. One of those girls could be a future friend.

"It looks like some kind of sports practice. And all the kids are covered up, Ibtihaj!" Mom said eagerly. But then Qareeb jumped into the car, and we had to pull out of the school yard.

"Qareeb, do you know what they're practicing there in the cafeteria?" Mom asked.

My brother shrugged and looked out the window, like he was thinking about the upcoming football season or all the homework he had to do that night, rather than my mom's question. "That's the fencing team," he finally mumbled. "I don't know anything about it."

Mom knew she was onto something, though. That night she went online and discovered that Columbia High School had one of the best fencing programs in the state, which was a significant honor because apparently New Jersey had the largest number of high school fencers in the country. Mom always did her research when something interested her—especially when it came to us kids—so she learned about fencing's history, too. She discovered that although many people claimed that fencing had originated in Europe, historians had found cave paintings depicting sword fighting in Luxor, Egypt, from 1190 BC.

Fencing also didn't originate as a sport; it was a method of defense used by soldiers in the military and enemies at war. Then in the fourteenth and fifteenth centuries, Europeans began to think swordplay was a fashionable and necessary part of a gentleman's education, and it stopped being only a method of battle. Instead it was a show of athleticism. With the invention of the wire-mesh helmet and a sword with a blunted tip, accidental deaths and injuries became less common, and fencing was featured in the first modern Olympic Games in Athens, Greece, in 1896. It was originally a male-only sport, and women's fencing was not introduced into the Olympics until the 1924 games in Paris.

The more my mother read about the Columbia High School team and the sport of fencing, the more boxes it checked off her list. A winning team to be a part of? Check. A uniform where Ibtihaj would be totally covered without having to alter the uniform in any way? Check. An opportunity to participate in a sport that wouldn't require Mom and Dad to drive her to practice? Check. There was only one problem with fencing: No one in our family knew much about it. But that wouldn't stop my mother. There was never a problem she couldn't solve. By the time I came down for breakfast the next day, Mommy had tracked down the coach of the Columbia High School fencing team, and I had a private lesson scheduled for the following week.

Frank Mustilli was a legend in the local fencing community. He'd been a college fencing champion at Montclair State College during his junior and senior years, and both of his daughters were successful college fencers. In fact, there was talk that the older daughter might make it to the Olympics.

My father and I went to see Coach Mustilli on a Saturday morning. We parked in front of the coach's redbrick house, and before we could get to the front door, a short white man with thick, shiny black hair and wire-framed glasses, who was wearing a T-shirt and sweatpants, came out to greet us. "I'm Frank Mustilli," he said, extending a hand to my dad. And then he turned to me.

"How do you pronounce your name, young lady?"

"It's Ibtihaj," I said shyly.

"Ibtihaj," he repeated. "That's an interesting name. I like it. Now let's go get started."

The coach led us down his long driveway to the garage. The inside of the garage looked like a mini gymnasium. There were a bunch of swords balanced in a rack, a long, narrow strip painted on the floor, and some bright-red electrical boxes, which I later found out were used to attach cords to the swords to track how many points each fencer made.

"Come on over here, Ibtihaj," Coach Mustilli said. "We only have thirty minutes, so let's get right to it."

My dad found a chair in the corner and sat down.

"Ibtihaj, first lesson: Fencing is like physical chess; you have to be strong and strategic," the coach said. I nodded and tried to keep the words "strong" and "strategic" in the forefront of my mind, but my mind was racing. This was the first one-on-one lesson I'd ever had, and I didn't feel comfortable being so close to a man who wasn't related to me.

"You have to be quick," the coach continued. "Fencing is all about speed and agility. It's strategy, it's technique. And everything comes at you within a millionth of a second. You think you can handle that?"

That's a lot to process, I thought nervously. But before I could answer, Coach Mustilli grabbed a sword and demonstrated what a fencer should look like in action.

"This is the strip," he said, pointing to the long, narrow

red rectangle on the floor. "All fencing takes place on this strip. If you step off the strip or get pushed off, game over. Got that?" With his sword in the air, the coach proceeded to move back and forth on the strip in a series of lunges and quick steps, all the while jabbing and thrusting his sword forward and backward. I felt my eyes grow wide, and I sneaked a peek at my dad, whose face was emotionless. I turned back to watch the coach.

"Now let's show you how you have to move on the strip," Coach said. "Come stand over here with me."

I walked over to the strip and faced Coach Mustilli. I could barely look him in the eye. I felt incredibly self-conscious.

"Okay, Ibtihaj," Coach Mustilli started. "Here's what I want you to do. Put your right leg in front of you and then bend it, like you're doing a lunge."

I did what he said, but he wasn't satisfied.

"Straighten that back leg," he said.

The coach must have sensed my nervousness, because before he put his hands on my back leg, he announced, "I'm going to just adjust your leg here a little bit."

I flinched when he touched me.

I think my dad did, too. He definitely made some sort of noise in the back of his throat and shifted uncomfortably in his chair. But the coach seemed oblivious.

He continued on with his lesson, occasionally putting his hands on me to adjust my stance or to move my arm into the right position. It always felt weird. *I know this is just coaching and that didn't mean anything*, I told myself, *but, boy, I'm uncomfortable.*

Coach Mustilli taught me how to lunge forward and then scoot right back. Lunge forward and scoot right back. It all felt very awkward, and when it wasn't, it was just boring. There wasn't a lot of action happening. My body felt strange in the neutral fencing position, with my knees bent and pointed outward. I could also sense Abu's discomfort. He kept shifting in his seat every time the coach put his hand on my leg or waist. Because we both understood that Coach's adjustments were simply a part of the lesson, we didn't say anything. But it was still unusual and awkward for me, not to mention Abu. This kind of close interaction between unrelated men and women isn't normal for Muslims. So when the coach finally said our time was up, I let out a sigh of relief—and I know my dad did, too.

When we got home, my mom could barely wait for us to walk through the front door.

"How was it, Ibtihaj?" she asked me, a look of anticipation on her face.

I glanced at my father, who answered for the both of us. "Ibtihaj will not be fencing."

My mom looked confused. "Why, what happened?"

"That man had his hands all over her."

My mother turned to me for confirmation. "You didn't like it, baby?"

I agreed with my dad. "It was okay. I don't know," I said. "I didn't feel very comfortable in that garage, and it wasn't all that exciting."

My mom nodded. There was nothing more to talk about. So I headed for the stairs, knowing that fencing wasn't going to be the sport for me.

— CHAPTER —
4

A Team to Call My Own

You can be the lead in your own life.

—Kerry Washington

Even though I hadn't started high school, I knew I had to come up with a plan for college. You might think I was crazy for starting so young, but I knew I couldn't just sit around. I had to make things happen for myself, and that meant planning ahead.

One of my summer teachers agreed with me. When we finished our biology class at NJIT, Ms. Ramos told a story about a student with a 4.0 GPA. He'd been accepted into five great colleges but ended up not going to any of them because his parents couldn't afford the tuition.

"Don't become the next cautionary tale," Ms. Ramos said. "It is never too early to figure out how you're going to pay for college. Don't automatically assume your parents are going to figure it out for you, either."

I knew Ms. Ramos was right, especially in my case. Sure, we had a house with a pool, but a cop and a teacher didn't make a ton of money every year. With four other kids to think about, there wasn't going to be a blank check from my parents for my college tuition, especially if I wanted to go to a private university out of state. Mommy and Abu would be there to help—my mom even bought a giant book about college scholarships for me—but the work of earning that scholarship would fall to me.

Ms. Ramos had already made us come up with our wish list of colleges we wanted to apply to. Earlier in the summer we'd had a college fair, and I'd collected catalogs, buying into the dreams they were selling. I wanted to go to one of the schools with the best reputation that offered the best education, and I had settled on all eight schools in the Ivy League, plus Duke.

As I started to brainstorm how to get the most scholarship money for college, I again paged through my catalogs and noticed something. *Wait a second*, I thought. *All these Ivy League schools have fencing teams!* An idea sprouted in my brain, and I hopped off my bed, went over to my desk, and turned on my computer. While I waited for it to boot up, I tried to remember what I'd learned at that lesson in

Coach Mustilli's garage. I didn't recall much, only that it was really uncomfortable. I started typing in questions about fencing into the search bar on my computer, and one hour later realized I needed to give fencing another try. I knew my dad would be supportive because it was a high school team sport, not a private one-on-one lesson, and close to a year had passed since that tense session with Coach Mustilli. I'd emotionally matured a lot since then; now I wasn't confused about what overstepped the bounds of my faith. Fencing was also a purely practical decision. Ms. Ramos had told us to go after scholarships that we were uniquely qualified for instead of the ones that "everyone and their mama" were going to try to get.

I quickly devised my plan.

I had four years to become a good enough fencer to earn a scholarship. And, I figured, even if I didn't get a scholarship, it would still make me stand out on my applications. I noticed that almost all the fencers in the pictures I'd seen were white men, so being a young black female fencer would definitely make me an original. Like Serena and Venus Williams, maybe I could break down barriers and open up a sport to minorities like me.

My high school game plan also included taking all honor and advanced placement classes, plus staying active in athletics. There were different sports I wanted try, one for each season, because I knew colleges wanted to see a diverse resume. I was going to do volleyball in the fall because Damaris played it, fencing in the winter, and softball in the spring. Now all I had to do was convince a few friends to try out for the fencing team with me. That way, if I didn't like it, at least I'd be hanging with my girls.

Damaris was involved in another winter activity, so she was out. I settled on my friends Stacey and Ana, who'd come to Columbia from South Orange Middle with Damaris. We'd quickly become friends and were on the volleyball team together.

After practice one day I reminded Stacey and Ana that fencing tryouts were coming up. "All we have to do is show up for the first day of practice, and essentially we're on the team," I said, trying to make it sound fun and easy.

"Do we really want to do this, Ibti?" Ana looked at me like I'd asked her and Stacey to go to the dentist with me.

"Yeah," Stacey added. "Maybe fencing's not for us?"

I couldn't figure out why they were so skeptical. Stacey's dad had fenced in college, so he loved the idea that she might check out the team. And Ana's mom wanted her to try out, too. So as far as I was concerned, that left both Stacey and Ana with little choice in the matter.

"Aren't you even a little bit curious what fencing is like?" I pressed.

Both of my friends shrugged.

"Don't worry, Ibti," Ana said. "We love you, and we'll be there. But if it's lame, I'm out."

"Yeah," Stacey said, locking arms with Ana. "Me too."

On the day of tryouts Ana, Stacey, and I met outside the school cafeteria. All of us were dressed in gym clothes. I had on my gray sweatpants, Stacey had on some cute purple Nike shorts, and Ana wore capris. We looked ready. Before we walked into the cafeteria, Ana asked me, "Ibti, aren't you hot in those baggy pants? It still feels like summer."

"No, I'm fine," I said, brushing it off with confidence. But inside I was thinking, *I've been justifying how I dress for years. Can't we just drop it?*

"I'd be sweating if I had to wear long pants all the time. I don't know how you do it," she added.

"It's not that big of a deal," I said, firmly this time so they'd let it rest. "I'm used to it."

Stacey must not have been listening to me, because she picked up where Ana left off. "I could never be a Muslim because I am always hot. Plus, I look too cute in tank tops."

We all giggled, but I cringed on the inside. I didn't really care that I wore hijab. Modesty was what my faith asked of me, and it was how my mom, sisters, and I had always dressed, so I never secretly longed to run around in a bikini or short shorts. The issue was that it was hard to feel different, especially around my best friends, and harder still when people made a point of it.

"Come on, you guys, let's get in there," I said, changing the subject and hoping to get my friends excited.

I pushed the door open to the cafeteria, and the three of us peeked in. There was a *huge* crowd of boys and girls—a hundred at least. Most of them were white and kind of dorky looking. At first glance it didn't look like a welcoming space for three black girls with something to prove. So we turned around and let the door close behind us.

Stacey and Ana looked at each other and almost in unison said, "No way!"

I laughed. "Come on, you guys. Let's just check it out."

"Sorry, Ibti," Ana said. "We've only been in high school for two months, and we are not going to kill any chance we have at having a normal social life by joining that team."

I turned to Stacey. I couldn't believe she was going to just walk away from this opportunity. *We can be on another team together!* I thought. *We have this great chance to try something new and hang out, and you haven't even given it a chance!* But instead I just frowned and whimpered, "Come on, it could be fun."

Stacey scowled. "You cannot make me go in there, Ibti."

I couldn't believe they were ditching me. But then again, lately it seemed a lot of my friends from school and my neighborhood were more interested in being cool, making sure they were hanging out with the right people, and thinking about boys. Me? I was the same Ibtihaj I'd always been. I still liked riding bikes, playing with my Barbies, and walking down to Main Street to get ice cream. Chasing boys and going to high school parties weren't even options in the Muhammad household anyway.

"Why don't we all try out for the track team instead?" Ana said. "That way, we wouldn't be the only black kids on the team. And we wouldn't be associated with those guys in there," she said, gesturing toward the nerdy-looking white kids in the cafeteria.

At that moment I knew I had to make a choice: follow my friends or stick to my plan. I thought about trying out for the track team, and my mind immediately went to the uniform. What would I have to wear? Then I thought about the comments my friends had just made about my clothes, and imagining what people who didn't know me would say clinched my decision. I was going to stick to my plan because my plan was going to take me places.

"I'm going to try out, you guys. I'm sure it won't be that bad," I said.

"Suit yourself." Ana shrugged, giving me a quick hug to show me her decision wasn't personal. "We're leaving. Come on, Stacey."

I knew they didn't mean to hurt my feelings, but I still felt a mixture of anger and disappointment as I watched my friends leave me to face the fencing tryouts alone. "I'm going to get into a good college, you'll see!" I half yelled at them, mostly joking. But I think I was trying to convince myself as much as them.

I marched into the cafeteria and found the sign-up sheet.

Coach Mustilli didn't say anything to me as I stood in line with the other kids. I figured he didn't remember me. The coach and the team captains didn't waste any time trying to make nice. Within minutes of the official start time, we were running hall sprints, and doing frog jumps and bear crawls until sweat was pouring from every inch of our bodies. I never knew I could work that hard, and these were just the warm-ups!

"I had no idea fencing would involve so much training," I said to a freshman girl I'd passed in the hall a few times.

"Me neither!" she said, wiping sweat from her face with a hand towel. "This is harder than cross-country!"

Almost an hour later we got to the fencing part. After an explanation about the three different types of swords fencers can use—épée, saber, and foil—we were told to select one. "It doesn't matter to me what weapon you choose," Coach Mustilli said.

I wasn't sure which weapon I wanted, but another freshman girl I knew from math class chose épée, so I did the same. When I picked up the sword, it was lighter than I expected. The blade was stiff, and narrow near the end. I was surprised to find what looked like a blunted smooth button at the tip of the sword instead of a sharp point. Clearly, no one was going to draw blood with this weapon!

"Excuse me. Can I ask you something?" I said to a confident-looking girl who seemed a little older than me. "Is épée a good choice for a beginner like me?"

"It is," she answered. "Good luck today!"

Problem solved.

After explaining that if we got on the team, we'd have to purchase equipment or rent it through the team's rental program, the coaches sent us over to a small storage shed to find protective gear to wear. They called the uniforms fencing whites. I also needed a jacket, half jacket, glove, and chest protector. Finding equipment that was my size and didn't smell like sweaty gym socks took time, and there were so many layers it was hard to figure out which piece to put on first. I had to watch the older kids demonstrate more than once. For the lower-body fencing uniform there were pants called knickers, long white socks, and special fencing sneakers. We were allowed to practice in our regular sweatpants, so we didn't have to wear the knickers. On our heads we had to wear the special wire-mesh masks that Coach promised would protect us from losing an eye. The mask felt weird on my head at first, but I was so happy that it fit comfortably over my hijab.

"I feel like a mummy," the girl from my math class said. "Am I going to be able to breathe in this thing?"

I didn't say anything because she and everyone else would probably have thought I was crazy, but once I was all suited up, I was so happy that I blended in—even if we all did slightly resemble mummies.

The coaches then divided us up by weapon. I followed the épée group back into the cafeteria, where we were broken down into smaller groups of ten or so based on our experience.

The more-seasoned fencers got started with their drills right away, and I watched them moving back and forth on the strip the coaches had marked off on the floor with masking tape. I was blown away by the fact that they could jab their sword and hit their target with such precision. To me, those kids looked like they were fighting for real. They weren't the same meek students I saw in the hallways or sat next to in class; they were dueling opponents battling for victory.

That wasn't what I remembered from my lesson last spring in Coach Mustilli's garage. If fencing had looked this exciting, I would probably have kept at it. I turned my attention back to the coach. Coach Mustilli was working with the saber students, so those of us in the épée group worked with an assistant coach. His name was Jason, and he had recently graduated from New York University (NYU), where he'd fenced for their team.

On that first day, I and the people in my group barely touched our weapons. After we took off our helmets, we had to learn basic fencing footwork: how to advance, retreat, and lunge. What sounded really simple, moving forward and backward, was actually quite difficult. The legs had to be shoulder distance apart, with the front foot facing forward and the back foot perpendicular to the front. Legs bent at the knees, we awkwardly advanced down the strip in this position over and over. Toes up first, then land on our heels. It was like I was learning how to walk all over again, trying to keep my balance in this awkward position, while simultaneously trying to forget how much pain my legs were in. Once we got a handle on the footwork, we finally got to pick up our weapons. Jason told us to hold our épées steady, with the tip of the blade pointed out in front. Then we were to lower our left hand behind us and lower our stances even more. I tried to follow his directions to the letter, but I felt a shooting pain through the front of my right quadriceps and down the back of my left hamstring.

Ouch! I thought as I winced and grabbed the front of my right leg.

"It feels awkward, I know," Jason encouraged me. "But you'll get used to it. I promise."

I wondered if "awkward" was a synonym for "the most painful thing ever" in the fencing world, but I didn't say anything.

I looked around at the other underclassmen. Everyone had a look of serious concentration on their faces as they struggled to get the moves right. Some kids giggled nervously as they tried to maneuver their bodies into these "awkward" new positions, but no one was laughing at anyone else. No one was talking about anything but fencing. It was only the first day, but already we felt like a team.

Very quickly fencing became a big part of my life. Coach Mustilli demanded it. Just by showing up, I was effectively on the team, and there weren't really cuts because so many kids dropped out after the first few challenging practices. In addition to training for almost three hours after school every day, we also had practice on Saturday mornings from nine to noon. Some kids on the team competed in the local and regional competitions as well, and those were held on Sundays.

Intense but endearing, Coach Mustilli motivated the team with his focus and drive, and that was what he wanted. "Commitment and hard work are what separate champions from everyone else," he'd always tell us. Then he'd warn us that if we didn't want to put in the time, we didn't need to be on the team.

Practice was methodical and tough. We usually started out with a warm-up run and group stretching led by the team captains. If anyone showed up late to practice, the whole team had to do sprints down the length of the hallway adjacent to the cafeteria. If ten students were late, we had to run ten sprints. No exceptions. We trained as a team, we won and lost as a team. Everyone was treated equally, and you got out of the sport what you put in. We weren't black or white or Muslim or Christian; we were athletes. Even though I was the only Muslim on the team and one of only a handful of people of color, I always felt safe and like I was exactly where I belonged.

I didn't always feel that comfortable when we went to

other schools to compete, though. Fencing had a reputation for being an elite white sport, and often that was what the other teams looked like. All white students, white coaches, and white parents watching from the bleachers. I can't say for sure, but based on how nice their sneakers were and how well-dressed their parents looked, I think they were pretty rich, too. Our team of over one hundred fencers, with five black kids and two Asians, was considered a model of diversity in the world of high school fencing. As the only hijabi, I often felt all eyes land on me when I walked into a gym. There were times I couldn't wait to fence, just so I could hide behind my mask and blend in with the other athletes.

In a varsity meet, only nine of the team's best fencers compete—three in épée, three in foil, and three in saber. Each fencer has to fence three bouts, one against each of the members of the other team in the same weapon. Whoever scores five points first wins the bout, and the first school to win fourteen bouts wins the meet.

My first year on the team, I fenced only in the junior varsity meets. Not all teams were as large as Columbia's, so if there weren't any other underclassmen to fence, all of us JV kids were left to cheer on our teammates. But Coach Mustilli never made the kids who didn't get to fence feel like we weren't integral members of the team.

And while everyone knew who the top nine fencers on our team were, when the varsity team won, it was a victory for all of us.

When our team was winning by a sizable margin, which was more often than not, Coach Mustilli would substitute a few of the junior varsity members in for a bout. That's why we were always told we had to be ready to fence. That chance to be plucked off the sidelines and sent into action motivated everyone on the team to work hard.

By the end of my first season, even though I hadn't quite distinguished myself as the team's best épée fencer, I was in great shape. I could see muscles in my thighs and stomach where I had never seen them before. I could run four miles without even breaking a sweat. I felt confident and strong. I had a great new group of friends. And I had come to realize that while I enjoyed volleyball because I got to hang out with Damaris, Ana, and Stacey, I much preferred fencing because when I competed, I was acting alone. I was in total control of the outcome of the game. When I lost, I was the only one to blame, and I could train harder to do better the next time.

As my sophomore year finished, I still wasn't in the starting lineup, but I was a more confident fencer. I remember watching the newbies come in to practice and thinking how far I'd come since my days of learning how to hold my épée. When we had open fencing, where we were able to fence against one another at practice, Coach Jason didn't have to correct my fencing or footwork as much as he used to, and I could hold my own against some of the upperclassmen. Coach Mustilli was also letting me fence during varsity meets more often, especially when we were at larger competitions against more than one school. I didn't feel like I could put into words how happy being part of the fencing team made me. It was *such* a positive environment to be in. Even when practice was hard, we still managed to have fun. Most important of all, I fit in without having to try. It was the only sport I had ever participated in where I didn't have to wear something different. I could just be me, and for that reason alone I was more than willing to practice six days a week and work harder than I ever had before.

"Are you still going to play softball this spring?" Damaris asked one day. She knew I wasn't having an easy time getting along with the girls on the softball team.

I wasn't sure. My original plan was to play a sport each season for all four years of high school, but the softball team was tough. I was the only nonwhite person on the team, and the other girls generally weren't very friendly. When I compared playing softball with my experience on the fencing team, it was hard to find the enthusiasm to play a game I didn't love, with team members who made me feel like a third wheel.

"I don't know," I finally said. "Maybe I'll play this year and see what happens."

"A very diplomatic Ibtihaj Muhammad answer," Damaris said, laughing.

I laughed, too. "Hey, I gotta make sure I'm doing the right thing for my future. I'm not as cute as you, so I can't just depend on my looks."

She laughed right back. No matter what, it always felt good to have a friend like Damaris.

— CHAPTER —
5

Ready to Roar

If you're going to do something, you're going to do it to be the best.

—Colin Kaepernick

"Who made that noise?" Coach Mustilli demanded as he ran into the épée and foil practice room.

No one answered.

I finally raised my hand. "It was me, Coach."

"Ibtihaj, get over here," he yelled. I dropped my weapon and mask and ran over to Coach Mustilli. I had been free fencing with my teammate and screamed in happiness when I scored my winning point. It wasn't often you heard épée fencers shriek, especially at practice, but I was so excited I couldn't resist.

"Yes, Coach?" I said timidly as I approached him.

"Ibtihaj," he said, "I didn't know you had it in you. That's the kind of fire we want to hear and see."

I sighed in relief, but I was confused. *What is he getting at?* I wondered.

"I heard that roar all the way from the other room," Coach Mustilli said, grinning like he'd just unearthed a hidden treasure. "I came running because that is the sound of a champion."

I didn't really know what to say, so I smiled back and awkwardly waited for the coach to continue. I wasn't *really* a champion. The team was, having captured the state championship two years in a row, but I wasn't even a varsity starter. Instead I'd distinguished myself by being a hard worker and by always arriving to practice on time, ready to give it my all. It was why I had been voted captain this year, even though I was only a junior.

"I want you to come fence with the saber squad," Coach continued.

What? Saber? That was not what I was expecting. The last thing I wanted to do was switch weapons. I was finally one of the top épée fencers, and Coach wanted me to start all over from scratch? Saber was so different from épée. In épée, you scored a point by compressing the tip of the blade of the sword anywhere on your opponent's body, from the head to the toes. With saber, the target area was from the waist up, and saberists used slashing motions to score. Everything was a lot faster and way more aggressive than in épée. During competitions the saber fencers were loud and screamed on almost every point. Sometimes this was just to show dominance. Other times they did it because, in saber, attacks happened so fast that it wasn't clear who'd gotten the point. If someone screamed, it was as if she was trying to persuade the ref that it was, in fact, her victory.

"No, thanks. I like épée," I said to the coach politely.

Coach Mustilli stopped smiling. "Then you're off the team."

I seized up, unable to tell if he was serious or joking. "I don't want to get kicked off the team, Coach," I protested. "I just don't want to switch weapons."

"Look, Ibti," Coach Mustilli said, softening his tone. "All of our saber girls are graduating next year, so I need a new saber squad ready for next season. You'd be in our starting lineup."

"I *like* fencing épée," I tried again. I wouldn't dare say it out loud, but I also liked my épée friends. Over the last two years, practicing together, we had our own little group, and I didn't want to lose that.

Coach Mustilli rolled his eyes and took a deep breath. "Do you like winning?"

"Yes," I said.

"Well, the team needs you to win. We need a saber fencer, and you have what it takes to help this team repeat as state champions."

I felt a wave of anxiety wash over my body.

"But why me?" I practically whimpered. Maybe if he thought this idea through, he'd realize I wasn't his best option.

"Because I heard you roar," Coach said, as if it were obvious. "Only a saber fencer roars like that. I thought you were a meek little person in there, but you obviously have something else going on."

I didn't know if I should be nervous or excited by this new opportunity. But before I could say anything, Coach Mustilli added, "I know a star when I see one, Ibti, and you have the makings of a great saber fencer."

Wow, I thought. *Coach really believes in me.* But did I believe in myself? Did I really have the potential to be a great saberist? I kept coming back to all the extra work I'd have to put in. Did I have the willpower and patience to learn a whole new weapon? I would have to start watching saber bouts more closely—as soon as possible. But before I could ask any more questions, Coach Mustilli made the decision for me. He guided me out of the épée and foil room and took me to the cafeteria, where the saber fencers practiced. Then he turned to me and said with a wicked grin, "Welcome to the dark side."

We got right down to business.

Coach Mustilli started out by telling me that fencing saber was all about speed and strategy. "It's controlled accuracy," he said. "To master saber, you've got to make quick decisions and execute them just as quickly." This was very different from épée. "When you were fencing épée," he continued, "you were waiting around for just the right moment to make a move. You were reacting to your opponent. With saber, there is no waiting, Ibti. I need you to be a hunter."

I tried to keep up with Coach Mustilli's instructions, tried to grab on to some of his obvious passion for saber fencing, but I still didn't know if Coach had chosen the right person. I didn't see myself as a "hunter," and I didn't know if I was capable of the speed he was talking about.

"How will I know if I can do it?" I asked him. What I really wanted to know—and couldn't ask him—was what would happen if I failed?

"You don't have to know," Coach Mustilli said. "You just have to do what I tell you to do. Can you handle that?"

I nodded.

I didn't know if Coach Mustilli was crazy or just super enthusiastic, but something about what he said sent shivers of excitement up and down my spine. If the coach was right about me, that I could really excel at saber, I was all in.

The first time I held the saber, it felt a bit awkward. I had to get used to the grip—it was different from the épée—but I loved how light the blade felt in my hand. Pretty quickly I found the speed of saber fencing liberating. There were more ways to move and new means of getting points. Coach Mustilli reminded me I could use the sides of my saber blade to score, not just the tip, and that if I missed the target, I should keep my blade out in front of me on defense to control my opponent's attack. He showed me the major defense moves—the parries—I would need as a saberist, and he gave me a handful of DVDs of champion saberists to take home to watch. He told me to pay attention to their footwork more than anything.

Coach Mustilli worked with me one-on-one during practice for at least thirty minutes every day until he was confident he could turn me loose with the rest of the saber fencers. It took only about two weeks to feel like I'd been fencing saber all along. It came much more naturally to me than épée had, and I almost felt guilty that after two years of hard work on the épée squad, I had abandoned it with no regrets.

Early on Coach Mustilli called me over to fence with

Rachel Carlson, who was the best female saberist we had on the team.

"Okay, Ibti, let's see what you've got," Coach Mustilli said.

"But I don't know what I'm doing," I responded hesitantly.

"That's how you learn," Coach said with a sly grin. "Sink or swim. But I think you're going to swim, Ibti."

Coach told Rachel to grab me a lamé, a silvery-gray jacket that defines the scoring area on the fencer. The target area in saber is from the waist up. A lamé conducts electricity (though you can't feel it!), and a body cord extends from the jacket to a scoring machine. Once you're hooked up, points register when the blade makes contact with the metal mask or lamé. This is much different from fencing épée, where the tip of the blade needs to be compressed to score.

Coach told us to get on guard, or in the starting position. "Ready," he said. "Fence!"

Before I even knew what was happening, Rachel rushed at me, her sword slashing. She hit me with the side of her blade, and the coach yelled, "Point left," meaning Rachel, the fencer on his left, had scored.

I don't think I'd even moved out of the ready position.

"Ready," Coach Mustilli said again. "Fence!"

Rachel flew off of the on-guard line, and this time I

had the sense to retreat. She didn't stop, and pretty soon she'd forced me to the far end of the strip, where I actually fell backward to the floor. As I struggled to stand up, I was relieved my mask hid my face as I fought back tears.

"Stop," Coach Mustilli yelled. "Ibtihaj, where's your fire? Where's the fight in you? Get over here."

Rachel stayed on the strip, and I walked over to the coach, pulling my mask off my face. I wanted to remind Coach Mustilli that *he* was the one who thought I was full of fire, not me, but I held my tongue.

"Listen, Ibtihaj, I want to see the same speed I see when you're running sprints. The next time Rachel attacks you, I want you to be faster than her in the box. If you miss, that's okay. Do you remember how to control your opponent when she runs at you? Control the distance and her speed. Keep that blade out and in front of you!"

"Okay," I said, even though I was still full of doubt that I could actually do this. Rachel was being so aggressive I thought perhaps the coach should have me fence someone else.

Once again we were back on the strip. "Ready," Coach Mustilli said. "Fence!"

This time when Rachel launched her attack, I tried to remember her rhythm and speed. I didn't think about scoring, but rather how to keep her blade from hitting me.

I knew how fast she was coming, so I fought back quickly. But Rachel fooled me again, hitting me with a fast lunge underneath my right arm. I barely had a second to think before she scored again, this time using a different tactic. Everything was so fast. In épée I had time to feel my opponent out and was able to build my strategy during the bout. In saber I'd have to learn to think a bit faster on my feet.

"You're doing great, Ibtihaj," Coach Mustilli shouted.

I pulled off my mask in frustration. "Really? I haven't scored one point yet."

"Trust me. You're learning," Coach said with a grin. "Now do what Rachel did to you. Attack her and try to score a point."

Once again Rachel and I stepped to the on-guard lines, at opposite ends of the strip, masks on. I had to think of a plan fast.

"Ready," Coach Mustilli said. "Fence!"

Before I could attack Rachel, though, she rushed at me and scored an easy touch on my arm.

I turned to Coach Mustilli, ashamed. "Sorry, I wasn't ready."

He shook his head like he was disappointed. "Are you ready now?"

I nodded yes. *No fooling around now*, I told myself. *Do it.* Then I spoke up. "Ready."

"Okay, you two," Coach Mustilli said again. "Ready. Fence!"

This time I tricked Rachel. As soon as I heard the coach say "fence," I made two advances with my blade extended, immediately followed by two quick retreats. Rachel made the same fast double advances, this time followed by a lunge, with her blade swiping only the air, narrowly missing me. I then lunged, throwing my arm out, and my blade hit the top of her mask. The green light on the machine lit up. I had finally scored a point!

Coach Mustilli clapped slowly.

"Great action, Ibti," Rachel said from behind her mask.

"Thank you *so* much!" I said to Rachel, grinning with pride that I'd made the point, and grateful for what a good sport she was.

"Now we're getting somewhere," Coach Mustilli said. "Let's do it again."

This time I tried to use my speed against Rachel, and it worked well. My double advance lunge was a tempo faster, but I hit her on the thigh, off target, immediately realizing my mistake.

"Darn it," I said under my breath.

"You're fencing saber, not épée," Coach Mustilli shouted. "Remember you have to hit above the waist."

Coach Mustilli kept Rachel and me there fencing with

each other for the next hour, and I began to get the hang of working with my new weapon. As I learned Rachel's go-to moves, I started scoring more and more. Soon I wasn't afraid of getting hurt, but more concerned with accurately anticipating what Rachel would do. The intensity of saber had all my senses popping, and I swear I could feel the adrenaline pumping through my veins. For the first time, I actually felt like fencing was fun—not because I got to hang out with my teammates, but because of the sport itself.

Within just a few weeks of switching to the saber, Coach Mustilli added me to the varsity starting lineup. He also mentioned the idea of my entering some of the local and regional fencing competitions, like some of my teammates did.

"Ibtihaj, let me be very clear," Coach Mustilli said. "I never ever send a kid to a competition if they're not ready. And I wouldn't tell your parents to shell out their hard-earned cash to pay for the fees if I didn't think you were."

"But there's no way I'm going to win anything," I objected.

"It's not always about winning," Coach answered. "The more bouts you fence and the more experience you get with fencers from other clubs, the better you'll be."

That night I went home and, over dinner, told my parents about the coach's plans for me. It was one of the rare nights when everyone was seated around the dinner table. No one had a game, and Abu had the night off.

"Local competitions? What does that mean?" my mom asked.

"It means that I would sign up for fencing tournaments here in New Jersey on the weekends. Coach Mustilli said that doing well at certain local competitions could qualify me for the Junior Olympics at the end of the season." While they aren't connected to the actual Olympics, the Junior Olympics are one of the most prestigious national tournaments for fencers older than thirteen.

Abu finished chewing his mouthful of salad and asked pointedly, "How much does it cost?"

"It's not that much," I said. "The entry fees are only, like, thirty dollars per competition."

"And how many of these competitions would you be doing?" Abu asked.

"I'm not sure," I said. "I think there's, like, one competition every weekend, but I don't have to go to all of them." I didn't want to make it seem like fencing was going to cost more than it already did. My parents had purchased me my own fencing equipment after my first year on the team. When I switched weapons, they'd also had to buy a saber lamé, which ran another $150. A near

$700 investment wasn't a small sacrifice in our home, so I wore my gear with pride, like armor.

"That could really add up, Ibtihaj," Mom said, exchanging glances with Abu. "But we see how hard you've been working. You're passionate about this, and it's going to help you get into college. If it's something you and the coach think is important, we'll figure out some way to pay for it. And you can talk to Auntie and Uncle Bernard. Maybe they'll help out."

"Don't worry about the money," Abu interjected. "You let us handle that, and you focus on winning."

I smiled from ear to ear. I was so excited, but I didn't take for granted what my parents were doing. I knew we weren't rich; my mom worked summer school, and Abu often picked up security jobs to help pay for all our extra-curriculars. They never treated them like a financial burden, but they were also clear that we had to put forth our best effort. If we weren't giving 100 percent, they weren't going to invest either their time or their money supporting us. Ever since I started fencing, though, both of my parents could tell I was serious. I was all in, and true to their word, they were, too.

My first regional competition was in Hackensack, New Jersey, only forty minutes away from Maplewood. The tournament was held at a fencing club, and when we walked in the door, there were already tons of people inside. I could feel the butterflies in my stomach furiously beating their wings.

"Ibtihaj! Claire!" Coach Mustilli had spotted me and one of my teammates and was heading our way. Claire had already been to several local competitions and had just missed qualifying for the Junior Olympics the year before. We weren't good friends, but I decided in that moment to stick to Claire's side like glue.

"Relax," she told me. "You're going to do fine. Everything is going to go by so fast you won't have time to be nervous."

"I hope you're right." I sighed.

After getting changed in the locker room, Claire and I started warming up, doing the stretches we'd done a thousand times before at practice. I stole looks at the other fencers, and I saw some anxious energy throughout the room—girls fidgeting with their hair, tying and retying the laces on their shoes. *Whew!* I thought, suddenly reassured. *I'm not the only person here who's a nervous wreck.*

After a few warm-ups and drills, Coach took me over to the table to see if pools had been posted.

Unlike high school meets, these tournaments were all about the individual. Each fencer was put into a randomly selected pool with other fencers based on ranking. Because this was my first local tournament, I didn't have a ranking of any sort, so I was placed in a tough pool with the number one seed. Each pool had seven fencers, so that meant I would fence six bouts, each to five points. The number of bouts you won and the margins you won by determined your ranking after the early pool portion of the tournament was over. Then we entered the next phase of the competition, where the goal was to keep winning and advancing in an ever-shrinking round of fencers. First there was a round of thirty-two, then sixteen, then eight. After that came the semifinal rounds, and eventually the finals, where the last two fencers would fight for first and second place of the entire tournament.

"Here you are, Ibtihaj," Coach said once he found my name. "You're in the first pool, and you're going to be fencing another girl with no ranking. Her name is Melinda Grady. Do you know her?"

"No, Coach," I responded.

"Good. Because you don't want to go up against someone

you know. When it's your turn, I want you to let that tiger out and attack Melinda. If you get that first point in fast, you'll break her confidence, and then you can take those other points away from her."

The butterflies in my stomach started up again. I had to remind myself not to waste time being nervous and that the bout would be over in an instant. *Five points is nothing*, I tried to convince myself. *It'll be a breeze.*

"Okay, Coach," I said. "I'll try that."

Coach Mustilli shook his head and pointed his finger in my face. "Don't try. Do! Do exactly what I said and you'll win! Got it?"

"Got it, Coach."

I breathed deeply, put down my mask over my face, and fenced harder than I ever had before. I secured the points I needed, advanced through the pool rounds, and battled against some of the toughest, most aggressive fencers in the tournament. But I stayed focused, goal oriented, and determined, and I had the time of my life. That day I came home with a twelfth-place finish, which allowed me to start my official ranking and be seeded in the next competition. Considering I'd competed against sixty girls, I was thrilled. Claire finished in second place, which put her that much closer to making the Junior Olympics.

Theoretically, I could think about that competition, too, but I knew that was far off in my future.

When I got home that evening, both of my parents were waiting for me. "How did you do?" Mommy asked expectantly.

"I came in twelfth!" I said triumphantly. "Against sixty other kids," I added to make sure they understood what that meant.

"That's very good," Abu said, his brown eyes twinkling. "But who won?"

I knew he hadn't meant anything by it, but I felt my triumph deflate. *Abu just wants me to do my best*, I reminded myself. "I don't know her name, but she was from Hackensack. She was really good."

"Well, did you learn something from this girl from Hackensack? Maybe you could do some of the same actions next time. Remember, always pay attention to the winners."

I promised I would, and at practice and the local competitions I watched all the fencers who consistently did well, and took note of what techniques they employed on the strip so I could try to do the same. I watched their footwork, their attacks, and their defensive moves. Meanwhile, Coach Mustilli worked me harder than before, having me fence against the boys, who were typically a bit faster and more aggressive than the girls. I quickly became the best saber fencer on the Columbia High School team, and I watched my ranking rise at the local competitions. Often I came home with medals in my hand.

After winter break Coach Mustilli told me he wanted to talk to me in his office after warm-ups. As I led everyone through thirty minutes of intense exercises and stretching, I searched my brain, trying to think of what the coach might say. Had I done anything wrong? I couldn't think of anything.

"Ibtihaj, sit down," Coach Mustilli said when I got to his office.

I sat and tried not to let my nerves show.

"I'm looking at your rankings. Did you know you're only one result away from qualifying for the Junior Olympics next month?"

"I am?" I said in disbelief. I knew I'd been doing well at the local tournaments, but it had never occurred to me that I was in the running.

Coach Mustilli smiled. "Yes. All you have to do is finish in the top eight in one more competition. And I think you're more than able to do that. There are two competitions this month. If you don't do it in the first one, you can try the following weekend."

I couldn't believe it. All the other kids talked about

qualifying for the Junior Olympics like it was the peak of their fencing career. Here I was about to make it there when I'd been fencing saber for only three months! And I hadn't even realized that qualifying was within my reach!

One month later my mother drove me to Cleveland, Ohio, for my first ever Junior Olympics. I had clinched my spot at the last qualifying event in January, finishing in fifth place, and now I was on my way to compete against the best youth fencers in the country at the biggest tournament I had ever been to. I was so excited I could barely contain myself.

"I'm nervous, Mommy," I said somewhere between western Pennsylvania and Ohio.

"I know you are," she answered. "I'm nervous for you, too. I still can't believe you're going to the Olympics already."

"First of all, Mom, it's not *the* Olympics. It's the Junior Olympics," I said, laughing. I still had to pinch myself every time I stopped to think about how quickly I'd climbed within the national tournament circuit. But I didn't dwell too much on that because I knew I needed to keep up my confidence. Coach Mustilli had warned me that there were going to be the best of the best at this competition, and that since I was still so new to the sport, I shouldn't expect to go home with any medals.

When my mom and I walked into the convention center, I felt her squeeze my hand. *She's seeing what I'm seeing*, I realized. As I looked around, I was overwhelmed by the sea of white before us. I was used to going to competitions and being the only black fencer in the room, or the only Muslim fencer in the room, but there were thousands of fencers here, and almost all of them were white. Even the majority of referees were white. The feeling of otherness settled upon me, and I couldn't help but wonder if people were staring at me, wondering what I was doing in their world.

Snap out of it, I said to myself. *Don't psych yourself out.*

Because there were so many fencers competing at the Junior Olympics, the tournament was four days long. As with every other tournament I'd been to, we started with the pool rounds and then progressed to direct elimination bouts. The first two days of competition were to narrow those two-thousand-plus fencers down to a manageable sixty-four. Then the elimination bouts began. I had a goal for myself to make it into the top sixteen, which I'd made in my last few tournaments in New Jersey, and I didn't think my expectations were too high.

Unfortunately, they were.

I lost five of my first six bouts, so I didn't even advance

to the elimination bouts. Basically, I was finished with the whole competition before things even really got started.

I was embarrassed, humiliated, and demoralized, and I ran to find my mother when I lost. Tears streaming down my face, I threw myself into her arms and bawled. She tried to console me, but I couldn't hear her over my own inner monologue, hating myself for doing so badly.

"Ibtihaj, you tried your hardest," my mom kept saying. "There's no reason to beat yourself up like this."

"You drove me all the way here...," I said, unable to finish my sentence. "I have been practicing," I cried, "a lot."

My mother gently lifted my chin up, wiped a tear from my face, and asked me to look at her. "Ibtihaj, you've been doing saber only a few months. Keep working at it, you'll do better next time."

"There might not even be a next time, considering how badly I fenced today," I responded, which brought a fresh batch of tears to my eyes.

Suddenly she said something that made sense. "Maybe you should get a fencing tutor? When you need to get better at something, you have to find someone who can help you."

A fencing tutor? The idea didn't sound too bad, but I couldn't even think about my fencing future after my dreadful performance. I just wanted to melt into the floor and disappear, so I let out a deep sigh.

"Do you want to get back on the road early and call it a day?" Mom asked.

Part of me wanted to say yes. But I also knew I needed to see what the best junior fencers looked like on the strip, and I didn't want my mom to think she'd wasted her time bringing me all the way out here.

"Let's stay a little while longer," I said softly, wiping my nose on a tissue. "Is that okay?"

"It's fine," my mother answered, and we both settled into our seats and tried to find a bout to watch. I was scanning the floor when a flash of color caught my eye. I don't know why I hadn't seen them before, but on the far end of the convention center there was a group of African American kids in matching uniforms. I followed their line of black-and-yellow sweatshirts to see that they were cheering on a black fencer I hadn't noticed before. They were screaming and yelling with such passion that I knew they had to be a team.

I nudged my mom. "Look over there at all those black people! Who do you think they are?"

My mom turned her head to look, then she smiled. "I don't know, but it's nice to see them here. I was starting to think we were the only ones."

— CHAPTER —
6

Fencing Stronger, Climbing Higher

I just never give up. I fight to the end.

—Serena Williams

Sitting in the stands at my competitions, my mom soon heard from other parents that there was a place in New York City where black people fenced. After my woeful performance at the Junior Olympics, Mommy finally decided it was the perfect time to find this club, to see if it would help me improve. She did a little research and discovered a website for the Peter Westbrook Foundation.

Through sheer coincidence, around the same time a documentary about Peter Westbrook premiered in New York City. My mother felt that was a good sign, so she took me and Faizah on the forty-minute train ride into the city to see it.

Peter Westbrook's story was a fencing fairy tale that had unfolded right in Newark. Peter was the child of a Japanese mother and an African American father, and his mother raised him and his younger sister alone in a housing project in Newark during the 1950s and '60s. At a time when race relations were tense, Peter struggled, and his mother worried that without a father figure in his life, he would turn to the streets for answers. In Japan his mother's paternal heritage included a long line of men of the sword—samurai—who held an honorable role in society. Peter's mother wanted the same sense of pride for her son and thought fencing could offer it. More importantly, she felt it would be a safe space from the streets. Once Peter's mom found out there was a fencing team at his high school, she begged her son to try out for the team. Legend has it that he struck a deal with his mother. He agreed to try fencing if she paid him five dollars. His mother agreed, so Peter went to the team practice after school. Secretly, Peter enjoyed the sport, but he didn't tell his mom that. Instead he said he wasn't yet convinced. She offered him another five dollars if he went back, so he did. Week after week he kept collecting money, until he fessed up that he'd found his true passion in the sport. As a saber fencer, Peter excelled on his high school's team and was recruited with a fencing scholarship to attend New York University, one of the best collegiate fencing schools in the country.

Peter's stardom only grew from there. In his first year of college, he won the NCAA title for saber fencer. By the time he was a senior, he had become the national champion, an honor he would repeat twelve more times over the course of his career. In 1976 he attended his first Olympics. By his retirement from competitive fencing, he'd been to five Olympic competitions, winning a bronze individual medal in 1984. During the 1992 Olympic Games, he was selected to carry the American flag for Team USA.

It wasn't just his success as a fencer that made Peter Westbrook so remarkable, though, it was also the fact that he came from such humble beginnings and still managed to dominate a sport that had previously been reserved for the white and wealthy. He fought racism and classism in order to claim his spot among the fencing greats, which he did on his own terms.

Once he retired from competition, Peter didn't hang up his saber. Knowing how fencing had saved him from a life of dead ends, he decided he wanted to help other young kids without a lot of advantages. Peter created the

Peter Westbrook Foundation in 1991 in Midtown Manhattan. The idea was to use fencing not only to teach the sport, but also to teach life skills to underserved children from the New York City area. What started as a small program for less than a dozen kids ballooned into a powerhouse operation serving more than 250 kids from the community, plus an elite program created to train young athletes with potential to fence on the national and international circuits. Pretty soon the Peter Westbrook Foundation had developed an international reputation as the place where good fencers of color went to become great.

When the film was over, I had tears in my eyes. Our stories were so similar. We both were born in Newark. We both were rarities in fencing—Peter for his race and I because I wore hijab. Peter had reached a level of success I only dreamed about, but I still felt an instant kinship with him. There was a reception after the film, and we had a chance to meet Peter and some of his foundation coaches. I was so nervous when I approached this wiry, bald-headed, older man, and I didn't know what to say when it was our turn to shake his hand. Luckily, my mother didn't have the same problem.

"This is my daughter Ibtihaj," she said confidently as she gestured toward me, "and she's a saber fencer at

Columbia High School in Maplewood. She's looking for a way to improve her game."

Sure enough, Peter told my mom to bring me to the foundation on any Saturday morning and they'd be happy to see what I could do.

Mom and I took the train into New York City in May, toward the end of my junior year of high school. We walked seven blocks from Penn Station to Twenty-Eighth Street and Seventh Avenue. The Peter Westbrook Foundation was housed on the second floor of a large commercial building, and we took the elevator up. When we got off, we entered into a huge, open space. The smell of sweat and metal hit us as soon as we walked in, and the sounds of chatter and fencing blades clanking filled the room. My mom and I paused in amazement. This was the largest fencing club I'd ever been in. There were some white, Latino, and Asian kids also on the floor, but the overwhelming majority of students seemed to be black or brown.

"Can you believe this?" I whispered to my mom, still in awe.

Everything around me seemed like a dream. Fencers that looked like me. Coaches that looked like me. To walk into a room full of fencers and not feel like the odd one out, to not feel eyes surveying my body, pausing at my hijab, wondering if my race or religion would prove an impediment to my success on the strip, felt like freedom.

"I know," my mom whispered back, her eyes wide. "This is going to be great. I can just feel it."

I recognized some of the Olympic fencers I'd seen in documentaries and videos we'd watched during practice. And they were standing only ten feet away from me.

"You must be Ms. Ibtihaj Muhammad," a man said as he walked over to us from the center of the floor. "Welcome to the Peter Westbrook Foundation. My name is Jerry."

"Hello, Jerry. I'm Ibtihaj's mother. We're here to get Ibtihaj some extra training, and we've heard great things about your program."

"Thank you," Jerry said. "Your coach, Frank Mustilli, goes way back with Peter, so we're delighted to have one of his students here. Come on in."

Jerry instructed me to get changed, and I went into the locker room and came back out in my full fencing kit, holding my mask in one hand, my saber in the other.

"Come over here," Jerry said, beckoning me to an empty strip. After I did a quick warm-up, another girl who appeared to be my age and height trotted over. "This is Angela," Jerry said. "We're going to have you fence with her and see how you do."

"Okay," I said, excited to see another black female fencing saber. I was trying to size Angela up, wondering how good she was. I knew immediately that I wanted us to be friends. But first we had to fence, and only one of us could win.

Angela and I assumed our positions on opposite sides of the strip. Knees bent. Sabers up. When Jerry yelled, "Fence!" I didn't wait for a second. I exploded out of the box toward Angela. I moved so fast she didn't have time to react. I scored a point, finishing quick, underneath her right arm.

"Point left!" Jerry cried, gesturing toward me and smiling.

"Thank you," I said from behind my mask.

"Ready," Jerry said, telling us to take our positions. "Fence!" This time I let Angela rush me, which I knew she would, but I blocked her blade with a parry, then hit her with a swift motion to her mask.

"Point left," Jerry yelled again. I smiled, knowing no one could see my face behind the mask.

After a quick match, with me scoring all five points, Jerry dismissed Angela, and another girl took her place. After I easily took her out, Jerry said he had one more girl he wanted me to fence. Again I scored all the points, and the girl walked from the strip just as fast as she'd walked on.

I took my mask off and allowed myself to breathe, but Jerry wasn't done with me.

"Brandon, come over here," he called, and a kid who looked about my age came running over. I sized him up and figured I could take him. I was used to fencing against boys during our school practices, so I put my mask back on and assumed my starting position. A small crowd of other coaches had now gathered around, but before we could start, Jerry called over Peter Westbrook. Suddenly my knees felt weak. I was going to fence in front of the legend himself!

I didn't let myself panic, though. I knew I could do this. I waited for the command, and when Jerry yelled, "Fence!" I didn't wait to see what Brandon was going to do. I started off quickly from the on-guard line, accelerating to a fast lunge around Brandon's parry. Coach Mustilli called that a number twenty-one. He had numbers for all the different tactical moves he taught us, so that when we were at a meet, he could shout a number to us and we'd know what to do. I now planned my bouts in numbers, which kept me focused. Brandon was a decent opponent, but I still bested him, scoring the winning point.

I felt triumphant, but Peter wasn't smiling at my victory. He looked at me skeptically, like maybe my win was just a fluke. Then he had me fight two other boys before taking a break. I beat them both, too.

"Ms. Muhammad, I can see Frank Mustilli has taught you well," Peter finally said.

"Thank you," I said, panting.

Peter told me to go back and change and then meet him over by the front desk. When I came out of the dressing room, I could feel the strain in my leg muscles, and my right arm ached. I walked slowly over to where my mother was sitting. Peter was already there talking with her.

"Here's what we're going to do," he said. "We have about two hundred students coming in here every Saturday for fencing lessons, but Ibtihaj here is beyond that. Frank's doing well with her. We'd like to have her join our elite group of students who come in to train after school. You have to promise to work hard, and in exchange we'll waive your membership fee, we'll give you your own locker, and when we think you're ready, we can help with the funding for tournament expenses. How does that sound?"

"That sounds good," my mom said. "But will she be working with you directly, Mr. Westbrook?"

"Ms. Muhammad," Peter said, focusing all his attention on my mom. "I'm here every single day on the floor with all the kids. Ibtihaj will have her own special coach, but yes, I will be overseeing everything that goes on here. Nothing happens here without my say-so."

My mom seemed satisfied with that answer, and I did, too. The energy that filled that room was palpable, and I wanted to be a part of it, to fence with other athletes of color and learn from Olympians and Olympic hopefuls alike.

In fact, I felt like I'd just won a prize. Shivers ran up and down my back, and I started to count in my head how many days and weeks it might be until I got to come back. I knew joining the Peter Westbrook Foundation could help me achieve my goal of landing a college fencing scholarship, but it would also help me develop into a better fencer, ensuring a better result than at my first Junior Olympics. I shook Peter's hand and officially became a foundation fencer.

I started training at the Peter Westbrook Foundation during the summer before my senior year. The daily routine was always the same. Upon arrival, I would join the group class, where we would do footwork and drills. We would spend a lot of time on technique, practicing a footwork series or a particular move over and over, so that at game time we would be able to execute instinctively. Once class ended, after about an hour and a half, we would have open or free fencing, which involved fencing with others or taking individual lessons with a coach. Every once in a while, mostly on Wednesday nights, Peter would watch us fence. Peter was a ball of energy as he walked around, either cheering our last attack or correcting our failed attempt to score.

Sometimes he'd interrupt a bout and push one fencer to the side so he could take his or her place and demonstrate exactly how an action was to be done. Even at fifty years old, Peter was still nearly flawless, exhibiting the fastest handwork I had ever seen. While he coached us on, he loved to apply Bible verses to fencing, his booming voice explaining how we could improve based on a certain scripture's teaching.

All that summer I loved the atmosphere at the foundation, and the people there felt like family. I quickly made friends with the other fencers, and when we weren't competing, we would be laughing and poking fun at one another. Sometimes I fantasized about going to school at NYU, just so I could keep fencing at the foundation and maybe even work there on Saturdays as an instructor.

When school started back up in the fall, however, it became harder to fence at the foundation. My schedule was brutal. College applications were due. I felt a lot of pressure to perform at the highest level in sports and academics. In addition to maintaining an A average, taking all honors and AP classes, and playing on the volleyball and fencing teams, I had to go to the foundation three days a week, plus Saturdays. I'd eat my dinner on the train, and once I got to the club, I would take a lesson, free fence for a bit, then catch the 8:50 PM train back home. Even though I'd want to do nothing more than fall asleep on that train, usually I'd take advantage of the ride to study. When I got home, everyone would be getting ready to go to bed, and Abu would be preparing to leave the house for the night shift. I'd say a quick hi, dash upstairs for a shower, finish my homework, then fall into bed.

When the month of Ramadan arrived during the season, I had to fast from sunrise to sunset. Not eating all day was never easy, but it was an important part of my religion, meant to direct my thinking away from worldly pleasures and toward Allah. I'd faithfully observed Ramadan every year since I could remember, and I was devoted to it. Through it all, I played volleyball and fenced, and I didn't want to take a break from either sport. The truth was, I was having fun, spending time with people I loved. The way I looked at it, giving up either volleyball or fencing would mean giving up not only an opportunity to develop my athletic abilities, but also a chance to spend time with my closest friends.

For the second year in a row I was captain of my high school fencing team. Fall sports previews thought we'd be state champions again, and as Coach Mustilli had predicted, I was now one of the best saber fencers in New Jersey. In February, I qualified for the Junior Olympics, and this time the competition was in Colorado. I flew there along with some friends from local high schools and teammates from the foundation. It was the first time I'd been out of New Jersey on my own. I finished in the top thirty-two, but a blizzard hit the same day we were due to fly home. I was stuck in Colorado for three days. While I knew my family was worried about me, and I missed them, my friends and I had great fun living in a five-star hotel, watching the winter wonderland from our windows and pretending school wasn't waiting for us back home.

My day-to-day life as a top student athlete felt like a car ride where my foot was always pressed firmly on the gas. But I had gotten used to the speed. My parents had instilled in me a strong work ethic and a nothing-but-the-best mentality. They had me convinced that if I was willing to work for it, anything was possible. For me, that meant getting an acceptance letter to a top university.

"She only got into Duke because she's black." I'd heard Heather Clark and her two best friends talking about me as I walked past them in the hallway. I knew they were referring to me because I was the only person from my graduating class—black or white—going to Duke University in the fall. Ultimately, Duke had beaten out NYU and Columbia as my top choice because they offered me the largest academic scholarship and because they recruited me to be on their fencing team. I wasn't sold on going to North Carolina, which felt so far away from everything and everyone I loved, but I couldn't turn down an amazing opportunity. As an African American hijabi, I didn't know what kind of welcome I'd receive in the South, but I figured that on Duke's campus I'd be in a safe environment where I would surely be able to find my "people."

Heather's words lit a fire inside of me. As I walked down my high school hallway that week, I was burning with frustration. I debated whether it would be worth it to let Heather and her friends know that I had earned the right to go to Duke with excellent grades in honors and Advanced Placement classes *and* as the captain of the fencing team. My college essay was about how I didn't let my race or religion stop me from getting ahead in a world that wasn't kind to people who looked or worshipped like me. As much as I wanted to educate those girls about my reality, I knew it wasn't worth arguing with ignorance.

Heather Clark wasn't the only person who gave me grief about going to Duke. My fencing family at the Peter Westbrook Foundation had made their own plans for me. They wanted me to stay in the New York area so I could continue training at the club. Even though I'd gotten into NYU, Peter's alma mater, the financial aid they offered couldn't compete with Duke's. I promised Peter that I would keep up my training at Duke and planned to come home during all my school breaks to practice. But they still weren't thrilled with my decision to leave them behind.

The truth was, I was looking forward to having a break from the foundation, and it was because of my coach.

When I first heard that Sam Jones was going to be my coach, I was excited. Not only was Sam a US Olympian alongside Peter, but he was also black and a Muslim like me. I hoped we'd have a real connection, but from day one something was off. Maybe Sam felt uncomfortable around me because I wore hijab and he was a less conservative Muslim. Maybe he just didn't like my personality. Whatever the reason, there was tension between us, and I never knew what to expect from him when I came to practice.

I remember one day I came out of the locker room, ready to work, and Sam gave me an irritated look.

"You didn't say hi to me when you came in, so you can go home and try again tomorrow," he said gruffly.

My face drained of all its color, and nausea washed over me. *Why would he say something like that?* I thought angrily. But I knew from past experiences not to question Sam, because that would make him more upset. So I said nothing, marched back into the locker room, got dressed, and headed for the door. When Peter saw me in my street clothes, he stopped me.

"Where are you going, Ibtihaj?" he asked.

I told him what Sam had said.

"Go get changed," he answered matter-of-factly. "You're staying right here for your lesson. I'll talk to Sam."

For the second time in less than fifteen minutes, I headed to the locker room and got ready for practice.

These kinds of bizarre mind games were commonplace when working with Sam, and I wasn't the only one who dealt with his strange behavior. One day Sam sent two girls home from practice, telling them not to come back until they'd lost ten pounds. Another time he told me not to come to practice unless I brought him a fifty-dollar box of Titleist golf balls. When I complained to some of the other coaches at the foundation about him, nothing seemed to change, so I let it go. I just did my best not to provoke him. My parents had some idea about Sam's odd behavior, but I didn't want to give them any reason to stop sending me to the foundation, so I forced myself not to complain at home. I admit, I didn't really know how to handle an irrational and easily irritated adult. I was young and inexperienced, and my coach was an Olympian. So I told myself that since my lessons with Sam were usually only thirty minutes out of a two-hour practice, I could stomach it.

Because of that, I was ready to continue my fencing career somewhere I didn't have to deal with coaches like Sam Jones. And I was excited to start my studies to pursue my career in medicine, closing the chapter on my old life, turning a new page.

7

College Life

Women are intersectional human beings who live multi-issued lives.

—Linda Sarsour

IBTIHAJ MUHAMMAD, 2005 JUNIOR OLYMPICS NATIONAL CHAMPION. I ran my fingers over the inscription on the trophy that sat in my college dorm room. Two days before, I'd scored the winning point and secured the gold at the Junior Olympics tournament in Ohio. It was an amazing moment, the peak of my fencing career. I should have been thrilled, but I couldn't muster up that feeling anymore.

"What's the matter?" my roommate Kendall asked. "You're over there moping like you lost your best friend, and you just won that big ol' trophy. Why aren't you out celebrating with your team?"

I sighed and tried to plaster a smile on my face. I didn't have anyone to celebrate my win with. The sad, lonely truth was that after a year and a half on the fencing team at Duke, I could call only one teammate—Josh—my friend. Now that I was in college, basically a grown-up, having male friends was spiritually acceptable for me. Josh was the only other black person on the entire squad, and the only person who made me laugh. He tried to get me to take fencing less seriously, but I didn't know how to be anything but serious when it came to sports. I had an unapologetic intensity that not everyone understood.

I didn't think Kendall needed to hear all of that, so I said the first thing that popped into my head.

"I don't have time to celebrate, Kendall," I said, which was true. "I have that chem test on Monday, and I didn't get a lot of studying done on the plane ride back from the competition."

"Well, I guess that means you don't want to go to Central Campus. Me and Tesia and Sandra are going to a step show."

"Thanks, but I can't" popped out of my mouth on autopilot. As much as I would have liked to go hang with my roommate and the other girls from our dorm, I knew there wasn't enough time. There never seemed to be enough hours in the day to fit a social life into my schedule.

"You sure?" Kendall said. "You know you need to have a little fun once in a while."

Before I could figure out another nice way to say "thanks but no thanks," someone knocked on our door.

"Open up," a giggling voice called.

Kendall jumped off her bed and flung open the door. Tesia and Sandra stumbled into the room laughing. They were both dressed for a night out. Tesia wore black leather leggings, a red shirt, a tapered denim jacket, and black high-heeled strappy sandals. Sandra wore dark denim jeans, a purple blouse, and similar strappy sandals, only hers were gold.

Sandra came over to my bed. "Ibtihaj, why don't you come with us? You need to get out, girl."

I smiled. "First of all, I wouldn't even know what to wear to hang out with you three."

"Well, not if you wear that tired Duke hoodie," Tesia said, and everyone—including me—laughed. Even though I didn't hang out with these girls on the weekends, we were a tight bunch of black women who lived in the dorm together, and I appreciated the sisterhood we'd formed. On a campus that was mostly white, it was nice to have women who looked like me nearby.

"I'm making an executive decision," Kendall declared. "You're coming with us and I don't want to hear any more excuses."

I looked at the chemistry book on my desk and then back at my friends. I slipped on a nice pair of jeans and a fashionable but modest top. It wasn't a hard choice. My friends won.

Two hours later I was wondering why I had agreed to come out. The evening had started out so well, too. We'd gone to a step show and watched a bunch of guys from black fraternities compete for bragging rights as the best steppers on campus. Then after the step show Sandra swore she knew about a small party that was happening that was going to be "totally low key." If "low key" meant pumping music and throngs of people, then that's exactly what it was.

"Really, Sandra," I screeched when I saw crowds of people pumping their fists in the air as they danced together. "This is not low key in any way!"

"Oh, Ibtihaj, you needed this," she said. "Trust me. You are going to thank me in the morning."

Pretty soon Tesia and Kendall went off, making small talk with people they had met around campus. I stood in the hallway and tried to figure out where to train my eyes, how to stand so I wouldn't attract attention.

"Hey, Ibtihaj!" A guy named Mark from my dorm came up to me. "You wanna dance?"

I felt my face flush but knew Mark wouldn't be able to see the color in my cheeks because it was so dark in the room. I didn't want to tell Mark that I couldn't and didn't dance with guys. So I just said "No thank you" as politely as I could.

Mark simply shrugged and moved on. I was grateful he didn't press the issue. After Mark, a couple of other guys came over to talk to me. Most were nice enough, but one wasn't; he just wanted to tell me he'd never seen a Muslim at a party before.

I couldn't have felt any more out of place. I squinted and scanned the room, looking for a familiar face. I decided I'd put in enough time at this party and it was time to leave. I brought my phone up to my face: 10:30 PM. As I started moving through the crowds of people, I saw my roommate close to the door.

"Hey, Kendall," I shouted, "I'm going to head home."

Kendall's brow wrinkled up in concern. "Are you sure? We just got here."

"I'm okay. I just have to go home and study."

"Really, Ibti. You're going to study? Now?"

I couldn't help but laugh. I *was* going to force myself to get in an hour with my biochemistry textbook, but that wasn't what was making me hightail it out of that party. I didn't feel comfortable, and I was clearly making other people uncomfortable as they walked past me in my hijab, standing quietly to the side while other people danced. I saw people doing double takes and then whispering to their friends.

"I don't need to be here. You guys have fun. Tell me if I miss anything good." And with that, I left the building and headed out.

Back in our room, I wouldn't allow myself to feel bad for trying out the "normal" college student experience for one night. Sometimes I just wanted to fit in, hang out, and be like all the other girls in my dorm, but I could never quite get it right. I wanted a lot of things: to do well in my classes, to qualify for the National Collegiate Fencing Championships (or the NCAAs), and to spend time with my friends. But I couldn't fit academics, fencing, and socializing into my schedule. And I was still struggling to figure out how to be social in a way that aligned with my faith. College parties clearly weren't it.

I unwrapped my hair and forced myself to sit at my desk with my biochem book in front of me. I willed myself to read. Yet I kept staring at the bookshelf Janice, Kendall, and I shared. I looked at the books we'd accumulated in the last six months. Between the three of us, we'd amassed an impressive collection of books written by twentieth-century black female authors. Toni Morrison, Alice Walker, Octavia Butler, and Zora Neale Hurston were all represented. Just thinking about an African American literature class I'd taken made me wish I were writing a paper about Alice Walker instead of memorizing formulas and definitions. I went back to my desk and tried to dive into science, but I was getting nowhere.

"This stinks," I said to the empty room. "Why can't I study something that I'm actually interested in?" Then I paused and realized something. I didn't *want* to study biochemistry. Not only that, I had no desire to take any more math and science classes. I wanted to read more books and learn more about African American history. I wanted to discover where my people had come from, where I had come from, and what contributions black people had made to American civilization and society. But I couldn't just drop my plans to be a doctor, could I? I had been working toward a medical career for my entire life, and my parents would be so disappointed. If I majored in African and African American studies, what would I do after graduation? There wasn't a clear career path.

The next morning I woke up feeling uneasy about the idea of dropping my medical school plans, but I didn't have time to dwell on it. So I shoved the thought to the side and told myself I would worry about it later.

I had weight training, then I had my academic classes, followed by fencing practice, which ran from 3:00 to 7:00 PM. Competitions were generally over the weekends, and we usually had to travel out of state for those. I also had a part-time work-study job—calling alumni to ask them for donations to the Duke Annual Fund—that was part of my financial aid package and provided me with spending money.

Most of the time I functioned on autopilot and moved through my schedule with practiced determination. But this time was different. Something was really nagging at me and holding me back. Sure, I missed being home and with my family, but I spoke to them all the time, and my homesickness always passed quickly. The sinking feeling in my gut was due to the fact that I *hated* my major and career choice. I wasn't happy about the plans I'd laid for my future—at all.

A few weeks later I made one of the most important

decisions of my life. Despite my best efforts to convince myself that being a doctor was my destiny, I decided to double major in African and African American studies and international relations, with a focus on the Middle East, as well as minor in Arabic. These were the subjects I was truly interested in studying, and I realized that being a doctor had really been my parents' dream—not mine. When I told Mommy and Abu that I was ditching my plans to be a doctor, they were surprised because I'd always been so career focused, but they still said they would support me in whatever path I chose.

"If there's one thing we know about you, Ibtihaj," my dad said to me over the phone, "it's that you always come out on top."

"Yeah, we're not worried," my mom added. "We trust you."

My major life changes didn't stop there, though. After nearly two years on campus, I hadn't found a social group to call my own. I'd always been too busy to think about it, but lately it felt like there was a huge hole in my life. I realized I was losing my connection to Islam, and I missed my Muslim community back home. Even though there hadn't been many Muslims in my high school, we'd had a diverse Muslim community in New Jersey. At Duke, I was literally the only hijabi on campus, and usually I found myself practicing my faith alone. My first interaction with the Muslim Students Association as a freshman hadn't resulted in the warm welcome I'd expected. As the only hijabi and one of only two black Muslims in the group, I felt like an outsider. The female upperclassmen did not approach me or make any real efforts to be my friend, so I went to the meetings only sporadically my first year.

I'd always prayed at set intervals five times a day, but lately I'd found myself praying when classes felt too hard, when the members of my fencing team were giving me a hard time, or when I was homesick. I found myself looking forward more and more to Friday prayers, which happened just after noon and were the most important prayers each week. *Jummah* was held in the student center, and there were people there from Duke's undergraduate and graduate schools, as well as from around the community. But I didn't want to be a Muslim who turned to Allah only when I needed something. I needed to center my faith, and I knew having a smaller, focused community could help me do that.

I realized that I really liked practicing my religion in a tight-knit group. And even though the MSA was an organization with far more men than women, and still had zero other hijabis, I knew that it wasn't about what other people could bring to my life. It was what I wanted for myself. And what I wanted was a Muslim community that I could pray with and have fun with. I needed a safe space where I could be social, but I didn't want "being social" to involve anything that would compromise my faith. I wanted friends, but I needed them to be the *right* friends.

I promised myself I'd join the MSA, hoping to use it as a source of inspiration, clarity, and centeredness on campus.

The following fall, just a few weeks into junior year, I finally had a social routine that revolved around my Muslim friends. I spent every Thursday, Friday, and Saturday night with members of the MSA, doing everything from bowling to volunteer work in the community. If I had competitions, or if practice ran late, I'd have to take a rain check on the MSA. More and more I found myself wishing it were the other way around, though. I wanted to skip practice so I could hang with my friends.

In contrast to the MSA, the Duke fencing team didn't give me a feeling of well-being. In fact, it mostly caused me anxiety. Every year since joining the team, I'd been to the NCAAs, had been named All-American, and was almost undefeated on the collegiate circuit. But there were only one or two people on the team who shared my work ethic and had achieved the same level of success. Unlike me, my teammates thought it was okay to miss fencing practice to study for a test. I never made those excuses; I went to practice *and* studied hard.

But my problems with the fencing team were bigger than that. My friend Josh and I were sometimes the target of "harmless jokes" and offhanded comments about the color of our skin. Our teammates thought it was funny, for example, to ask us if we liked to eat fried chicken and watermelon for dinner. Josh was furious, and he eventually decided fencing wasn't worth that type of abuse. He quit the team before my junior year.

One time after Josh quit, the team traveled by bus to a competition at Notre Dame. We made a pit stop to eat at a Cracker Barrel restaurant, and as we stood in the entranceway of the restaurant, waiting for a table, the hostess came over and offered to find a table for two— for me and the bus driver, who happened to be black. She must have assumed the two of us were together and not part of the fencing team. Everyone on the team burst out laughing, and not a single one of them spoke up to correct the woman's mistake. The experience perfectly exemplified how I felt on the team in general. Like an outsider. Separate. Different. Out of place.

"I'm going to quit," I said to Josh, who was telling me for the eleventh time how great his life was since he'd left the fencing team.

"You? Quit fencing?" Josh laughed. "I'll believe it when I see it."

"What? Isn't it possible I want what you have? Being a college athlete eats up all of your time and energy. And I'm done feeling different because I'm Muslim and black on a team that's all white. I'm ready for a real life—like you have now."

Josh responded carefully. "You're not like regular people, Ibti. You have some kind of superhuman ability to work two hundred times harder than anyone I know. You win on the strip and still manage to get good grades while double majoring. You wouldn't know what to do with yourself if you stopped fencing."

I laughed. "Yes I would."

"Oh yeah, like what?" Josh asked, cocking his head to the side and crossing his arms.

I didn't want to admit to Josh that he was probably right. I didn't know what I would do without fencing, and that was the only reason I didn't quit. Luckily, my financial aid package didn't require me to fence, so I was free to make a decision without worrying about my tuition. Fencing had been a part of my life for so long. But I also couldn't imagine spending another year with people who made me feel uncomfortable in my own skin. So I shrugged and mumbled, "I'd find something. I mean, I have three years of lost time to make up for."

"Like I said," Josh repeated, "I'll believe it when I see it."

Josh's words haunted me because he had identified the real reason I was still on the team. If I wasn't Ibtihaj Muhammad the fencer, who was I? The other big problem was I didn't really have anyone to talk to who could truly understand my dilemma. I didn't want to call anyone back at the foundation, because they would say, "We said you should have gone to NYU." Of course, there was no one on the fencing team at Duke who had my best interests at heart, and Josh, who understood me better than almost anyone, hadn't really helped me.

So with the burning desire to leave the fencing team and make a change, I decided to call my parents and ask them if they would help fund a summer study-abroad trip in Morocco. There I could further my North African studies and practice my Arabic—all while earning college credit. I knew it was a bit drastic, something that students with athletic commitments rarely considered, but studying abroad was an opportunity too good to pass up. My parents thought so, too, and even though it was tight for them, they agreed to cover the costs.

I didn't know what would be waiting for me back at Duke when I returned, but I figured no matter what, I'd be better able to deal with it after time away and some perspective.

In the capital city of Rabat, Morocco, which sits right on the Atlantic coast in the northwest corner of Africa, I lived with a Moroccan host family and took classes at the Center for Cross Cultural Learning in the medina, or old city. I immediately felt a connection to the Moroccan people because we shared the same faith, and I was overjoyed not to be stared at everywhere I went. Not to have to explain myself to anyone. For the first time in my life, I wasn't a minority. In fact, I probably experienced less culture shock in Morocco than I had when I first arrived at Duke!

Sometimes I did feel overwhelmed, like when my senses were bombarded by the chaos of the shopkeepers in the medina, or when I got lost in its winding streets. Or when I smelled baking bread and sweet spices mixed with the coppery scent of meat being chopped by butchers, or when I felt far away from my family. There was a constant background noise of motorbikes roaring, and I never stopped hearing voices speaking Arabic, a language I was desperately trying to become fluent in.

After spending the morning in our intensive Arabic and Moroccan culture classes, my American classmates and I would play volleyball at the beach until the sun went down. On the weekends our Moroccan friends would take us surfing, or we would go on train trips up and down the coast. Moroccans were so nice, and the food was delicious—not to mention halal. That summer I was carefree, and for the first time in a long time I allowed myself to enjoy not having a timetable or real commitments. It was such a difference from my life back at Duke, from the life I'd been leading since I was thirteen. My majors were no longer abstract areas of study; they were what I was living, eating, and breathing every day for three months. My mind was stimulated, my spirit was full, and I rarely thought of fencing.

Toward the end of my time in Rabat, as I sat on the beach looking out over the crashing waves of the Atlantic, as the sun painted the sky pink and purple, I thought about what I wanted my life to look like when I returned to college. I made a mental list of what I would prioritize—things like community service and charitable work were on the top. Even though my time in Morocco had been better than I could ever have imagined, many times I had come face-to-face with extreme poverty and suffering, and I realized how privileged I was living in the United States. I knew I wanted to help other people when I returned home. I also knew I wanted to continue studying and speaking Arabic so I didn't lose the knowledge I'd gained in Morocco.

Suddenly I realized my "What I Want in Life" list didn't include fencing. When I thought about the Duke team, my stomach clenched and a wave of dread passed over me. I curled my toes into the sand, closed my eyes, and tried to imagine my life at Duke without fencing. Rather than the blank canvas I'd feared during my conversation with Josh, I saw myself volunteering with the MSA, shining in my classes, and having time for my own pursuits. I felt relaxed, and when I opened my eyes, I knew I had made a decision.

When I returned to Duke for my senior year, I immediately told my fencing coach that I would be leaving the team. He took it pretty well, considering I was his best female saber fencer. He understood my desire to have at least one year of college when I could focus on something besides fencing and my classes. But even if he had wanted to, my coach really couldn't have done anything to stop me from leaving. I hadn't signed a contract, and I wasn't fencing on any scholarship, so I was free to go.

As I had imagined on that beach in Rabat, my senior year was full of happy, carefree me time. I played pool with members from the MSA after Friday prayers, I went to the mall in Durham with my friends, and sometimes I would just hang out in my dorm room listening to music. For the first time at Duke, I prioritized my personal happiness, and that helped me figure out what was important to me.

By the time I hit graduation, I felt confident and comfortable with who I was—both as a black American woman and as a Muslim American woman. I had a deep understanding of African American history, and my faith had evolved to include the things in life I believed were important. My interests and activities no longer required my parents' approval, too, and I decided it was okay to do things that my parents didn't feel fit with our faith, like listening to popular music. I had proven to myself that these things did not alter my obedience to Islam.

Despite some bumps along the way, I felt like Duke had given me an excellent education in mind, body, and spirit. I graduated knowing so much more about myself and my history, and I left with a sense of pride and appreciation for my identity that I didn't have before. By the time graduation rolled around, I'd decided I wanted to go to law school, with a specific focus in international law. Hey, it wasn't med school, but it sure was close! I planned to work for one year while I studied for the LSAT, then I would apply to law school. I didn't know exactly where I would land careerwise, but I knew taking things one step at a time was the way to go.

As soon as I had my diploma in my hands, my parents and I packed their car and headed home. I was ready for the real world! As for fencing, I figured that part of my life was over. I hadn't fenced competitively or trained for almost a year, and I had no intention of hopping back on the strip. Fencing had gotten me all the way to an elite university, just like I had planned, and now it was time to move on.

— CHAPTER —
8

Surviving the "Real World"

If you have no critics you'll likely have no success.

—Malcolm X

I took the elevator to the twenty-third floor of a Manhattan skyscraper and smoothed the pleats on my pants. I'd picked out what I thought was the perfect outfit for an interview: black trousers, a blazer, a gray pin-striped blouse, and black heels. I felt and looked the part of a corporate executive. I wore little makeup, and I carried a black leather briefcase with copies of my résumé. When the elevator doors opened, I put on a businesslike smile and walked over to the woman sitting at the reception desk.

I was interviewing for a paralegal position at a prestigious law firm. I was excited for this opportunity because this firm did a lot of international business in the Middle East and Europe, and they had offices all over the world. I could already imagine myself being transferred to the Abu Dhabi office and using my Arabic. I was getting way ahead of myself, but I knew I could kill it at this job if given the chance.

"May I help you?" the receptionist asked me.

"Yes, I have an appointment at ten thirty with Craig Finch in human resources."

"Name?" she said sharply.

"Ibtihaj Muhammad." I mouthed my name slowly.

She looked straight at me. "Can you repeat that, please?"

I did.

"Just a minute." She then picked up her phone and talked into it. "There's a woman with the last name Muhammad here to see you. She says she has an appointment at ten thirty."

Without making eye contact, the woman told me that Mr. Finch would be out in a moment, and then she pointed me toward a seat. I thanked her, trying not to take her frostiness as a bad sign. This was New York, and people were known for not being very friendly. As I sat there in a stiff chair and tried not to sweat, I reviewed my talking points, reminded myself that I was more than qualified for the position, and sent a quick prayer to Allah that this time would be different. This time I would get the job.

In the three months since graduation, while studying for the LSAT, I had dutifully sent off dozens of résumés to law firms, major corporations, and financial institutions in New York and New Jersey. So far I wasn't having much luck. Very few people were even calling me back. Most of my friends were in grad school or had found great jobs, but not me. Everyone said it wasn't my fault; it was the economy. College students couldn't find jobs, and thousands of people were being laid off from long-term careers. While I knew all this was true, it didn't make me feel any better. I simply wanted my life to *start* already.

Finally a tall, blond man who looked to be in his midthirties came through the glass doors into the reception area. He walked right over to me and held out his hand.

"Ms. Muhammad, I'm Craig Finch. Thanks for coming in today."

I stood up, took his hand, and smiled. "Thank you."

"Why don't you come with me, and we can get started."

I grabbed my briefcase and followed him to his office. To get there, we had to walk through a maze of cubicles and offices. I tried not to be obvious as I scanned the faces around me, searching for anyone who looked like me. I didn't see more than two people of color, and there were no other women in hijab. My heart sank just a little. This wasn't the diverse workforce I'd expected to see given the company's global profile.

"Welcome to human resources," Craig said as he led me to his corner office with views that showed off New York City's skyline. He gestured to the seat in front of his desk, and we both sat down.

"So, Ms. Muhammad," Craig said, "tell me a little bit about yourself."

I was ready for this open-ended question, so I began to talk about my academic achievements and my success in fencing. I told Craig how I'd studied Arabic at Duke and in Morocco, and then I emphasized my ability to work independently, with excellent time management skills. I stressed how much I wanted a career in international law, and how a job at this firm would be the perfect gateway into that field.

"That's all impressive," Craig said. "And I have to say you have a lot of the skills and attributes that we're looking for."

"Thank you," I said, smiling. I tried not to sound too excited, but inside I was feeling very confident.

"Now, as I'm sure you are aware, Ms. Muhammad,

this position is in a very demanding department. Everything is always an emergency or high stakes. There's no room for mistakes or accidents."

"Of course," I answered.

"And the lawyers you'd be working for are very exacting, and if they need you to stay at the office to work until two AM, then you have to stay late or come in on weekends. Would you be comfortable with that?"

"Absolutely," I said, nodding. "I'm known for my work ethic. I'm not afraid of working hard or being in the office all night, if that's what's required of me."

"Okay," Craig said, but there was an odd note of doubt in his voice. He paused and cleared his throat before continuing. "I'm just wondering if there would be any conflict with your, um, lifestyle choices that might interfere with the work we do here."

I didn't know how to respond. It is illegal for an employer to ask someone about his or her religion in a job interview. My religion was evident from my name and my hijab, so I knew Craig was referring to my being Muslim. But I didn't understand what he was implying.

"I'm sorry, I don't know what you mean," I said.

"Well, I'm just thinking that there are certain things about your, um, lifestyle that would prevent you from giving one hundred percent here in the office."

Now I was *really* confused, and honestly, I was angry, too. Without pausing, I blurted out, "Are you saying because I'm a Muslim, I won't be able to do the work here?"

Craig immediately threw his hands up as if to block my words.

"No, no, no. I would never say something like that. I'm just thinking that maybe some of the late nights here or working with certain people might be uncomfortable for you. For example, I'm wondering if your head wrap is something you wear all the time, because we do have a company dress code that is really strict, and you might feel out of place."

I was shocked. "Head wrap"? And why would I feel out of place? Why would being a Muslim prevent me from doing the work at a law firm? But if I wanted this job, I couldn't be outraged. I simply needed to explain what being a Muslim meant and what it didn't.

"Mr. Finch," I said in a reassuring tone, "I have lived and worked and gone to school with non-Muslim people my whole life. I don't feel uncomfortable in those situations."

"Right," he said, nodding, but I could tell he didn't believe me. Actually, he probably wasn't worried that *I'd* be uncomfortable. I'm sure he was thinking that his other employees would be uneasy around me.

After that, Craig Finch asked me silly questions, like where I lived in New Jersey and what my favorite class at Duke had been. But I knew my answers didn't matter. It was obvious that he saw only my hijab, not me. I kept a smile on my face as I responded, but I understood the interview was over. As we walked back to the elevator, I was sure that would be the last time I ever saw Craig Finch—and it was.

As I headed through Midtown toward Penn Station, my mind was swirling with emotions. *It's been months since graduation, and my phone's pretty much stopped ringing*, I thought. *But the problem is I can't* force *anyone to hire me.* Here I was in "real life," and for all my smarts and skills, I couldn't think of one single way to get what I wanted: a good position in corporate America. I'd even extended my job search outside of a desk job, applying to Teach for America—the national teaching organization that places college graduates in schools in underserved communities—but I was turned away after the third round of interviews.

Everything in my life was in limbo and out of my control. I was desperate, and when I thought of my future, I got queasy. I wasn't used to this level of powerlessness. As an athlete, I had known that if I worked a little harder, I could find success. As a student, I had known that if I struggled, I could find a tutor or take an extra class, and eventually I'd catch on. I didn't want to assume that my difficulty finding a job was because of my religion, my last name, or because I wore hijab, but I wasn't naive. It was at least *part* of the problem.

Ever since the September 11 attacks, Muslims in America had been looked at differently. On the morning that the Twin Towers were struck in New York, I was in the eleventh grade. The teachers turned the television sets on in my high school, and as we watched the horror unfold, all the Muslim boys, including my brother, were rounded up and isolated in one single classroom for the day. School officials said it was for their own protection, but it sounded like discrimination to me. From that day forward, it was clear that Muslims were seen as a threat in America. Hate crimes against US Muslims had more than quadrupled since 2001. Now it was 2008, and I considered myself lucky that I hadn't been a victim of violence, but the thought that I couldn't get a job because of my religion was disturbing.

I need to be in control of something—anything—in my life, I thought, *but what is that?* Then it hit me: fencing. When I stood on the strip, I knew what the rules were. I understood what I had to do. I knew I was good enough, and I didn't have to prove myself. If fencing could give me a small part of the day when I was doing something for myself, instead of waiting for the phone to ring, I was ready to give it another chance.

The day after the interview with Craig Finch, I took the train back into the city. As I stood outside the Peter Westbrook Foundation building, my limbs tingled with a sense of familiarity, like they longed to get back on the strip. At that moment I knew I'd come back to the one thing that had always been a constant and that had always inspired me.

Pretty soon I fell back into my old routine of going to the foundation four days a week. Most of the students I trained with were in high school or still in college, but I didn't care. I liked losing myself in a sport where I didn't have to think or plan for what was next. I just had to show up and work. On my worst days fencing was my therapy. If I woke up feeling aimless or uncertain about where my life was headed, I'd train harder so I could be certain I was the best fencer that day. In saber, I'd attack without mercy. I'm sure some of the other fencers didn't understand my competitiveness, but fencing was my only way to seek revenge on an enemy with no name. On the strip, I ruled. On the strip, winners and losers, enemies and friends, were well defined. In the real world, nothing was that clear or easy.

It took me only a little while to get back in shape, and

the physical exertion of training kept my mind off my failing job search. Soon fencing became my number one diversion, and I did it as much as possible. When I wasn't at the foundation, I would go to the gym close to our house and work out. I even competed in some local and regional tournaments. But there was one small problem with my new passion: fencing wasn't free or cheap. The Peter Westbrook Foundation was no longer investing in me because I'd aged out of their training program without reaching the national or international circuit. Basically, I was already considered a has-been, so Peter and his coaches were happy to have me around, but mostly as a training partner for everyone else. I had to pay for my lessons, competition, entry fees, travel, club membership, and equipment. My parents let me live at home rent-free—my father expected all his daughters to live at home until they got married anyway—but they made it perfectly clear that they would not be footing my bills, since I had a college degree. In their minds fencing was my hobby, and they were not in the business of bankrolling hobbies when they had to get Asiya and Faizah through the rest of high school and college.

One day, in a fit of desperation, I put in an application at the Dollar Store. Even the temp agency I had signed with had been unable to find me any regular work, so I had no steady income coming in. When I got the call from the Dollar Store that I had been selected for a part-time job as a cashier, I actually felt a moment of relief simply because *someone* had been willing to hire me. But those feelings didn't last long. Working at the Dollar Store was mind-numbing, humbling work. Customers were rude and dismissive, and every day I wondered why I had stressed over homework at Duke if the Dollar Store was it for me.

Soon, instead of searching the want ads for a job that paid more than the Dollar Store or studying for the LSATs, I was watching daytime talk shows until my mind went numb. I didn't know whom to talk to or ask for advice. I'd never been in a rut like this before. I felt so far from those days in Morocco, when I had a clear direction and plan for my future. Now I was adrift.

One afternoon my mom and Faizah walked in the front door, saw me in front of the TV, and exchanged a glance. I knew what it meant. It was the *Poor Ibtihaj* look that I seemed to be getting more and more these days. I hated being the object of pity in my own home, and I pulled myself up into a sitting position and rearranged my messy ponytail so I didn't seem so pathetic.

"Hey, you guys," I said, forcing myself to sound cheery. "How was school, Faizah?"

My little sister came to sit next to me. "It was good. I

had a fencing lesson with Coach Mustilli today. He said to tell you hi."

Faizah was only in eighth grade when she started taking private fencing lessons with Coach Mustilli in anticipation of being on the high school team. After watching my success in the sport, my mother had practically begged Asiya and Faizah to try it. Asiya had refused and settled on basketball instead, but Faizah was excelling at fencing. I was so proud of her.

"Did he ask anything else about me?" I blurted out, worried my sister might have told my former coach that I was working at the Dollar Store. For some reason it mattered to me that Coach Mustilli thought of me as successful. He'd made me believe I could do anything, and I didn't want him to see me as a failure now.

My little sister gave me a look. "No. He just said hi."

"Oh, good. Well, tell him I said hi back."

"You could go tell him yourself and see his new club," Faizah said, and smiled. "It's so much nicer than when you had to fence in the cafeteria."

I smiled back. Faizah was so sweet, and I knew she just wanted to make me feel better, but I didn't think I could face Coach Mustilli until I had a job.

I hauled myself off the couch and padded behind my mother into the kitchen. She told Faizah to go upstairs because she needed to talk to me. I figured she was about to give me another pep talk. My mother was a doer. She hardly ever sat still, and I knew seeing me on the couch every afternoon was making her crazy.

"Ibtihaj, I was talking to some of my colleagues at work, and they all think you should apply to be a substitute teacher," she said, while pulling pots and pans out for the evening meal. "You're so smart and good with kids, and it will pay you a lot more than the Dollar Store."

I scrunched up my face because of the way she said "Dollar Store." "Substitute teacher? I don't think that's what I want to do."

My mother stopped what she was doing. "Excuse me. Last month you needed to borrow money for your phone bill, so I wouldn't be turning my nose up at substitute teaching."

"I wasn't turning my nose up at anything!" I cried. "I just don't really see myself as a teacher."

"Do you see yourself as a cashier at the Dollar Store?"

"No," I said, and crumpled into my chair. "I didn't see myself not being able to find a job with a degree from Duke. I don't know what to do."

Mom pointed at me and spoke clearly. "What you can't do is give up. You have to keep trying things until a job turns up."

"I've been trying," I said, on the verge of tears. "And nothing is working. As soon as they see my name on my résumé..."

My mother made a soothing noise in the back of her throat. "Baby, you're going to be okay. I promise."

"I don't want to be just okay," I said as I started crying. "I don't want to be a substitute teacher or a cashier. I didn't work that hard in high school and college to be *okay*."

My mom turned away from me and went back to preparing dinner. "It's your life, Ibtihaj, and you're going to have to live it. I left the paperwork to apply for substituting on the dining room table."

I sat up and wiped my eyes. I could tell my mother didn't have time to keep trying to make me feel better. She had two other kids to take care of besides me. She didn't need any more of my moping around the house bringing everyone down. So I quietly left the kitchen, went back to the living room, plopped down on the couch, and turned the volume up on the TV.

A few weeks later I found myself at Coach Mustilli's new club, the New Jersey Fencing Alliance, which was only about ten minutes from our home. Ever since Faizah had told me that Coach Mustilli had said hi, I'd been nostalgic about how simple things were in high school. That had been a time in my life when I knew what I was doing and why I was doing it. I had felt invincible and self-assured. I was appreciated and supported. I would have given anything to feel like that again.

I quietly slipped into the club and was thankful that it was mostly empty. There was a coach giving a lesson on the strip, and I could immediately tell it was Coach Mustilli. His compact frame and booming voice yelling commands at his student made me feel at home instantly. When Coach was finished with his lesson, I gave him a nervous wave.

"Hey, Coach."

"Ibti, good to see you," Coach Mustilli said warmly, walking toward me with his mask in his hand. "I was hoping you might come by." We exchanged small talk, but soon there was an awkward pause in the conversation, and Coach Mustilli stared at me expectantly.

"What can I do for you, Ibtihaj?"

I wanted to say, "Can you help me make sense of my life?" Instead I settled for, "Do you think you could give me a lesson?"

Coach gave me a funny look, but he said okay. "Get your gear on."

I already had on sweats and a long-sleeve shirt, but I pulled a saber out of the rack of weapons near the front desk and found a spare mask and glove.

"Do some warm-ups," Coach yelled. I ran around the court a few times and stretched out my legs and arms. Part of me felt like I was wasting the coach's time with my request for a lesson—after all, I wasn't a fencing prospect for him—but I pushed those feelings aside because I needed to be in this safe space again.

We set up on strip number one, and Coach took me back through all my best high school moves. I easily parried and lunged and landed fluid, smooth attacks on my former coach.

Thirty minutes later Coach Mustilli was panting, but I was just getting warmed up.

"Coach," I said, half laughing but still serious, "can you give me a harder lesson?"

Coach raised his bushy eyebrows. "Okay, Ibtihaj, let's see what you've got." And then he let me have it, treating me like an equal opponent for the first time. He didn't hold back. He ran me up and down the strip, giving me the hardest lesson I'd ever had. I met him lunge for lunge, attack for attack. I was quick on my toes, and my saber sliced through the air as the sound of our blades clashing filled the room. I could feel the electricity coursing around me, like I was coming alive for the first time in months. I loved it. I was in control, and no one could take that feeling away.

Finally Coach Mustilli yelled, "Time!" We were both out of breath now. I took off my mask and smiled from ear to ear. "That was awesome, Coach."

He walked slowly off the strip and over to the tables. He got two bottles of water from his cooler and asked me to sit down. The sweat was pouring off his face now, and his hair was plastered across his forehead. He took a swig of water and leveled with me.

"Ibtihaj, what are you doing here? What do you really want?"

I was unprepared for this question. What *did* I want?

"What I saw out there," Coach continued, "was something I didn't know you had."

My eyes grew wide in surprise. "Really? You think I still have talent?"

"Talent? Ibti, I don't think you've even hit your peak yet. I think if you want to go all the way with fencing, you can."

I couldn't believe what I was hearing. No one had ever said this to me before. Not at Duke and not even at the foundation. Plus, I had never really imagined *anything* beyond college fencing.

"What do you mean, 'go all the way'?"

"I mean that you should think about competing on the international circuit and maybe even think about the Olympics," Coach Mustilli said. He must have seen my mouth hanging open, because he added, "I'm serious. I saw something out there today that I honestly didn't know you had."

I beamed inside and out. After all the recent rejections, this statement about my potential ignited a spark that I thought had long gone out.

"Don't thank me, Ibti," Coach Mustilli said with a warning in his tone. "If you decide to actually take up the challenge, it won't be easy. In fact, it'll be the hardest thing you'll probably ever do. Being a champion is a long, lonely road. You'll have to get up every morning, hungry, and you can't go to bed until you've exhausted yourself. And there won't be anyone on this path with you."

Even though I trusted Coach Mustilli, I didn't think he wanted to hear about the life crisis I was currently having. I didn't think he needed to hear that his words were feeding my soul.

"Do you think you can do it?" he asked, interrupting the jumble of thoughts and emotions running through my mind.

"Yes. I'm up for it," I said, quietly at first, and then I

repeated it to convince the coach, but also myself. Finally I had a real purpose.

"Okay, Ibti," Coach Mustilli said with a smile, "if there's anyone I know who has the strength and determination to do this, it's you."

"Thanks, Coach," I said, returning his smile.

"Don't thank me until you win. Until then your life is going to be harder than it's ever been before."

— CHAPTER —
9

Take Up the Challenge

Don't let the hand you hold, hold you down.

—Julia de Burgos

Once I committed myself to fencing again, my life became
a nonstop hustle to support my training. Because my paycheck from the Dollar Store couldn't cover my lessons
and still give me spending money, I had to figure out how
to make more—and do it fast. That's why I knew it was
time to rethink substitute teaching.

Being a substitute teacher not only paid relatively well,
it also allowed me to control my own schedule, working
only on days I wasn't training. Originally, I registered to
teach in my own school district, but my mom informed
me that I could make more money in the Newark Public Schools. I quickly landed a long-term sub position

teaching art history at the Malcolm X Shabazz High School in Newark. This school had recently been assessed as "one of the country's most troubled high schools," but I was willing to give it a try.

On my first day on the job, I walked into my classroom and tried to present myself as a confident, intelligent authority figure—but inside I was a nervous wreck. The thirty juniors and seniors in the classroom were only a few years younger than me, and I was afraid they wouldn't respect me. I had precisely one minute to prove my worth. After taking attendance, I asked the students to start reading their textbooks, per the instructions that their teacher had left. But half of them didn't even open their books. They just took up the conversations they were having before. When I asked one girl to please take out her book, she snapped, "I'm not reading anything in this class, and don't ask me again!"

I was shocked by the girl's disrespect, but I was also a little bit worried by the hostility of everyone in the class. I had known this job was going to be challenging, but this was worse than I imagined. No one wanted to do any work. The students wouldn't listen to me, and I didn't have the tools to make anything better. But I was committed to this job—and these kids—and I *had* to figure it out. So I talked to the principal and my mom, and I consulted with other teachers. Soon I realized that my role wasn't going to be teaching as much as making sure the students stayed in the classroom for forty-five minutes. It was more like babysitting, and sometimes I felt like an absolute failure. But I didn't have a whole lot of other options—except for fencing.

Three days a week after work, I'd hop on a train to Manhattan and stay at the foundation from five to nine. On the days I wasn't there, I'd be at the gym circuit training, working on my speed and agility. On Saturday mornings I would teach young kids at the foundation, which I loved because I felt like I was making a real impact on them, and I always remembered how influential my coaches had been when I was younger. In the afternoons I'd train more and take private lessons. I was a workhorse, but unfortunately, I didn't have much to show for it. I hadn't broken through on the domestic circuit, so my national ranking was barely worth mentioning. And my family and friends had begun to think I was crazy for focusing so much on fencing when I had a dual degree from one of the nation's top universities.

The other problem was that I didn't exactly know what I was hustling for. I couldn't visualize the prize because I didn't exactly know what the prize was. A spot on the national fencing team? Qualifying for the Olympic Games in 2012? Maybe. But how would I get there?

I began to realize that having Sam as my coach again at the foundation wasn't helping me get anywhere. Sam had me doing the same workouts I'd done in high school. I asked Peter if there was another coach I could train with, but he said Sam was the only saber coach with Olympic experience. In fact, he was the *only* saber coach at the foundation.

"But I need something more," I said to Peter as we sat in his office. "I want to go all the way with this."

"There's no one standing in your way. If you want to go all the way, that's on you."

"It's pretty obvious Sam isn't interested in my development," I added. "We've been working together for almost six months now, and every lesson is the same. I just feel like I'm getting nowhere."

"How old are you?" Peter asked, squinting at me as if he were seeing me for the first time.

"I'm twenty-three," I said, trying to keep the defensive tone out of my voice. By my age most athletes who were considered to have any real Olympic potential already had cadet, junior, and even senior national team experience under their belt. I didn't.

He pursed his lips. "Ibtihaj, I'm not saying you can't do it, but you've made it hard on yourself. No one here is going to stop you from chasing your dreams, but I don't know if it's a realistic goal for you."

My heart sank. My hero was telling me that it might be too late to follow my dreams. He didn't believe in me, and the foundation didn't think I could make it. Here I was doing everything I knew how to do, but I needed someone to tell me how to do it differently or better. If I really had the talent to be successful in the sport, like Coach Mustilli said, why wasn't the foundation taking my effort more seriously?

I considered leaving the foundation in search of a new coach, but I felt a deep loyalty both to the foundation and to my teammates there, who'd become like family. Leaving would have repercussions beyond losing the support, camaraderie, and goodwill of my friends—I felt like I'd be considered a traitor to the unspoken brother- and sisterhood of black fencers. So I stayed, but I knew something was going to have to change.

"You talk white!" The accusation came out like an insult, and that's exactly what it felt like.

"Yeah, Ms. Muhammad, you sound all proper when you talk," a boy named Terrance added. "Is your daddy white?"

I closed my eyes and drew in a deep breath. "No. The

fact that I speak grammatically correct English doesn't make me white."

"Dang, she do talk white!" another kid called out, and then the room erupted in laughter.

I desperately wanted my students to know that I wasn't their enemy, that we had a shared history in common, that they had descended from greatness and didn't have to ignore their education, but every attempt I'd made to get them to listen had failed.

"Okay, you guys, when you're finished having your fun and are ready to get back to work, let me know." I retreated behind my desk and plopped down, took out a book, and tried to read. But I couldn't drown out the sound of the students' giggles and mean remarks. I wouldn't give them the satisfaction of seeing that they had upset me, so for probably the hundredth time in less than a week I reminded myself that working at this school served a purpose.

One of the main reasons I continued to show up every day to Malcolm X Shabazz High School was because my father's mother, Louella (now in her eighties), had moved back to Newark, and her home was only a five-minute drive from the school. On my lunch break I would go check on her. On the afternoons I didn't have to go into

New York for fencing practice, I'd sometimes stop in as well. Soon those visits became the highlight of my day.

My grandmother always had wonderful stories to tell me about her childhood and what it was like raising twelve children alone. Abu rarely spoke about his early years, so these stories were all new to me. I loved hearing about where I came from and what my father was like as a child.

On some of my weakest days, when I wanted to quit teaching, or when my training left me sore and exhausted, I would visit my grandmother, and she inspired me to dig deeper into my own reserves of strength and press on with my own challenges. Her life story put everything I was going through in perspective. I didn't like to complain to my grandmother, thinking she didn't need to worry about my problems, but she knew I was having a hard time, and she'd reassure me.

"You're going to be okay," she'd say. "But you can't give up, because the minute you do, it all comes crashing down. How do you think I managed by myself all those years, with all those kids? Did I know everything was going to work out? No, I just never stopped."

I smiled. "You're so strong, Grandma."

"And you have my same spirit, Ibtihaj. You just keep moving forward, and don't take any mess from anyone who tries to tell you different."

Unfortunately, my grandmother got really sick during the time I was teaching and refused to go to the hospital. She was from a generation that avoided hospitals like the plague—she birthed all twelve of her children at home—and nothing I said or did would convince her to seek medical treatment beyond visiting her primary care doctor. All he could do was give her medication to ease her pain, not cure what was actually making her sick. So I supported her the best way that I knew how, by coming to see her more and more. It was crushing to know that my grandmother wouldn't be around much longer, and yet it felt like I had been placed there by Allah to help take care of her. I was so grateful I had the privilege of spending her last days on earth with her.

I decided to take my grandmother's words to heart, and I reminded myself that all the work I was doing to become a better fencer would eventually pay off.

The problem was, what other people thought bothered me. No one believes a career in sports is a "real thing" unless it's in the NBA or NFL, or offers a big paycheck. Some friends and family members thought I was crazy for choosing a sport like fencing, and then crazier for sticking with it. Sometimes I questioned what I was doing, but I had to shift my thinking and convince myself that the struggles I was experiencing served a purpose.

My parents smiled through it all, though, and never tried to move me away from fencing, and I loved them for not giving up on me. Charting this unknown territory on a leap of faith was paralyzing at times, and I couldn't guarantee that success was coming. Would I ever make the national team, much less an Olympic team? I heard judgment in the innocent questions people would ask: "How long are you going to be doing this?" "Are you still going to graduate school?" "When are you getting married?" That's when I would think about my grandmother Louella, and I would renew my promise to continue on my quest to be the best, with nothing but faith and courage in my heart.

One day in early 2009, almost a year to the day since I'd fully committed myself to fencing, something happened that completely changed the course of my career. So many new people had joined the foundation that we were in desperate need of another saber coach. Peter soon hired a former foundation fencer named Akhnaten Spencer-El.

Akhi was in his thirties, and he'd been on a few national teams as a kid, even qualifying for the Olympics in Sydney in 2000. I had met Akhi at the New Jersey Fencing

Alliance in Maplewood when he briefly worked for Coach Mustilli. Akhi had golden skin, a permanent five-o'clock shadow, and eyes that crinkled like crescent moons when he smiled. I found him to be easily approachable and always encouraging. He seemed invested in the development of his students, so I didn't hesitate to tell Peter that I wanted to switch coaches. I had grown tired of walking on eggshells around Sam and dealing with his mood swings. Lately Sam had been showing up to my competitions late, if at all, and dressed like he was going out to a party. Instead of wearing sweatpants and sneakers like most coaches, prepared to give lessons, one day Sam showed up in pink slacks, a pink shirt, a pink fedora, and pink alligator shoes. His outfit showed just how disinterested he was in coaching or in helping his athletes during competition, proving to be more of a distraction than an asset. No matter what, I figured Akhi would certainly be an improvement.

Without a doubt, he was.

"Ibtihaj, I think you could be one of the best fencers in the world!" Akhi said to me after our first lesson together.

"Really? Me?" I asked, my disbelief clear. It had been a year since my one-on-one lesson with Coach Mustilli, and I was now holding on to my confidence by a thread.

"Yes, you," he said, chuckling. "Who else am I talking to?"

"Okay," I said, grinning like a fool. *I like this man*, I thought. *He's always trying to put me at ease.*

"You have a really good sense of timing, and you're really fast," he said. "I'm going to have fun turning you into a champion, Ibtihaj."

I wasn't used to being praised by the coaches at the foundation for my skill or promise. More often than not, they seemed to see potential only in the male saber fencers. But here was one of the greatest saber fencers our country had ever seen telling me that he could turn me into a top fencer. I couldn't wait to get going.

"So, when do we start?" I asked, the smile still plastered on my face.

"Actually, our training is going to have to be put on hold for a minute because I need to take care of something," he said.

"What do you mean?" I asked.

"I want to be a certified fencing maestro, so I have to go through a certification course in Hungary, and it's about to get started," he said. "I don't want to be an assistant coach forever."

My world crumpled at the thought. "Hungary? Like the country Hungary?" I asked, unable to hide my disappointment. "How long will you be gone?"

"Three months," he said, grimacing, and I realized he

felt genuinely sad that he was letting me down. "But I'll give you some exercises you can do while I'm gone, and I'm sure Sam can continue to work with you until I come back."

I felt a chill go up my spine at the thought. If only Akhi knew what I'd been going through with Sam. Here I'd mustered up the courage to let go of Sam, and now I had to train with him again for three more months—after he knew that I preferred Akhi as a coach!

That night as I rode the train home, I had to try to psych myself up for working with Sam again. I prayed that he wouldn't hold it against me because I had chosen not to train with him any longer. But unfortunately, Sam wasn't that mature. He made it his mission to make my next three months unbearable. He routinely came to my lesson late or would cut my lesson short. He refused to invest his time with me, treating me like a chore or, worse, a waste of his effort. Sometimes I wanted to scream "What did I ever do to you?" But it wouldn't have mattered. I'll never know why Sam was so dismissive of me. My only guess is that he had a general lack of respect for women, which I'd seen in the way he treated other girls in the program. When I was younger, he'd always seemed to favor the boys in class, allowing them to stand in the front line as examples to the rest of us, or hand selecting male students for special activities that girls were never chosen for.

But I didn't let Sam deter me. I showed up early to every lesson, persevered through tough group classes, and was always the last to head home.

Akhi was back by the summer. Most fencers take a break from training in the summer, since the fencing season runs from October through June, but we got right down to business.

Working with Akhi was amazing, and he was as hungry as I was for success. As a new coach at the foundation, Akhi needed to prove he had what it took to turn athletes into champions. I was hoping to become his first success story, and my spirit came alive under his coaching. Finally I had a coach who was willing to climb on board my crazy workhorse train, to put in the hours and grind. It was such a welcome relief to have someone who not only rooted for me, but believed in me as well. But it wasn't only his positive attitude and willingness to put in the time that made my working with Akhi so different. He was also showing me a new side to the sport of fencing.

Until this point I had always been taught to fence defensively by reacting to my opponents. I was given methods and approaches to attack or defend and was told to execute these moves with speed and strength. Akhi had a different approach. He told me fencing was a mind game, so he taught me to fence tactically. We spent a lot of time watching videos of some of the world's best female saberists—some from Russia and others from Ukraine—and Akhi would break the matches down for me point by point.

"You have to realize that it's human nature to want to score," Akhi explained as his eyes lit with enthusiasm. "Even the best-trained athlete is vulnerable to a strong tactical game, so you have to figure out how to get into your opponent's mind. Let her think there's an opportunity, but you have devised a plan to score using that false action that your opponent has fallen for." I nodded to show him that I was listening.

"You have to use your strengths, Ibtihaj," he said, "like your sense of timing and explosive speed, to your advantage. And you must have a plan A, a plan B, and a plan C. Before every competition you have to know your opponent's strengths and weaknesses, and know how you intend to beat them."

I devoured everything Akhi said and faithfully tried to execute everything he told me through the weeks and months of practicing together. I had never had someone put that much time and thought into helping me develop as an athlete. Better than any other coach I'd had before, Akhi taught me that my opponents' strengths and weaknesses were as important as, if not more important than, my own.

To say things changed dramatically after I started working with Akhi would be an understatement. I started competing at domestic competitions, which were a whole different experience than my last competitions while I was at Duke. It was like the difference between playing college basketball and being drafted into the NBA, and I savored every moment. My training with Akhi paid off at them, too! In 2009 I had to pinch myself as I stood on the podium at US nationals, a gold medal around my neck. That victory put on me on track for my first national team.

By the end of 2009—a year since going back to the foundation—I had fenced so well in the domestic competitions that I now had a high enough national ranking to compete on the international circuit. In my wildest dreams, I couldn't have imagined that happening so quickly. But it did!

This World Cup competition was to take place right outside of London. My parents were worried about me traveling alone, but the coaches at the foundation assured them that I would be well cared for. They also reassured my parents that I'd never be alone because there was another young female fencer, Candace, in the competition. Candace also fenced saber and was one of my favorite people at the foundation. She was always the face of calm, which is good company for any competitor.

The tournament was held at a private boys' school in an area called South Croydon. Pulling up to the Whitgift School on the first of the two days of competition, I decided the school looked more like a prestigious college than any primary school I'd ever seen. The imposing gray brick buildings were the size of castles. Candace and I found our way to the school's very modern gymnasium, which didn't look anything like the gothic buildings surrounding it. Once we were inside, the sound of clanking fencing blades and the fierce yells of the competitors engulfed us.

My stomach-turning anxiety and paralyzing worry must have showed on my face, because Candace smiled and reassured me. "Don't worry, Ibtihaj."

Candace had been fencing saber from an early age, and she was a better fencer than me. Everyone at the foundation, including me, was waiting for Candace to qualify for the US national team. In order for that to happen, she would have to be one of the top four saber fencers in the country at the end of the season. I knew she was close, and I was praying for her to succeed.

"I'm so nervous," I said. "My stomach is doing flips."

"You're going to be fine, Ibti," Candace said. "We both are. We're going to show these people what two beautiful brown girls from the USA can do with a saber on the strip." I laughed. I was so happy to be here with Candace. I tried to capture some of her enthusiasm, bottle it up, and carry it with me into my matches.

There are usually two days in a competition. The first is used to whittle down two hundred fencers to forty-eight. On the second day those forty-eight fencers join the top sixteen seeded fencers in the world to compete in the elimination rounds. I liken the top sixteen fencers in the world to superheroes: insanely fast, mesmerizing to watch, and lucky enough not to have to fence in the first day of World Cup competition. I clearly wasn't there yet, so I had to fence in the preliminary rounds and hope I made it to the second day.

When I walked into the gymnasium on the first day, the talent I saw on the floor overwhelmed me. I watched women fill every available space, running, stretching, fencing, and warming up for the first World Cup of the season. After finding my pool number and strip assignment, I took note of what countries the other fencers were from, and then I tried not to psych myself out. After warming up together, Candace and I sat with each other as long as we could, before wishing each other luck and heading over to our respective strips.

Unfortunately, it didn't go well—for me or Candace. Neither one of us made it to the second day of competition.

I feel as awful as the first time I went to the Junior Olympics and lost so badly! I thought.

Back at the hotel Candace tried to cheer me up, but nothing was more devastating to my pride than going out so early. I started down a steep slope of feeling bad for myself, but Candace stopped me.

"Ibtihaj, you can't let every loss destroy you. There are going to be way more if you're trying to do this full-time, so you have to get used to this. Why don't we go watch the competition tomorrow?"

"Why, so I can feel horrible all over again?"

"No, so we can watch the fencers that we lost to. Let's take detailed notes, then work on those moves back in New York. We'll never get better if we don't learn from our mistakes."

I stopped packing and sat down on my narrow hotel bed, realizing this was exactly what my mom and I had done when I lost at the Junior Olympics. It was also what Akhi had instructed: that I should always know my competitors. I couldn't go back to him without some sort of feedback on how I could do better.

"You're right," I said, standing up. "I'm going to learn something from this."

The next day Candace and I got up early and headed back to the Whitgift School. We went armed with notebooks and pens and were ready to spend the entire day taking notes on every match and studying as many fencers as we could. For each athlete I watched, I made two columns, one for strengths and one for weaknesses. These were the same women I'd likely see at the next competition—women from Russia and China, Tunisia and Hungary—so I needed to be ready when I faced them on the strip. As I watched, it became clear to me that everyone had their own styles and techniques. I liked how all the French fencers had strong parries and could easily score after successfully blocking their opponent. I admired the speed the entire Korean team seemed to have and how fearless the Russians were no matter who was on the other side of the strip. It was all so inspiring. As the day wore on and my notebook pages became filled with my frantic handwriting, I found myself fired up to get on the strip again and apply what I was learning. I knew I was fast and strong, but now I had to be patient and learn to fence a smarter match in the face of pressure.

— CHAPTER —

10

Embrace the Pressure

Just believe in yourself. Even if you don't, pretend that you do and, at some point, you will.

—Venus Williams

"Ms. Muhammad, can I go to the bathroom?" I looked up from my lesson plan and considered my answer. Obviously, I should say no because class had started only five minutes ago, but if I denied her request, my student would likely go to the bathroom anyway and curse me out in the process. It wasn't worth the fight. Also, what if she really *did* have to go?

"Yes, you can use the bathroom," I said, sighing.

"Can I go, too, Ms. Muhammad?" two other girls called out, not even bothering to raise their hands. I tried not to let my frustration show as I excused them, too.

I had told the students that as long as they were reading and/or sitting quietly at their desks, I wouldn't force them to actually do the work they had been assigned. It hurt my heart to see that for most of the kids in the classroom, reading meant playing with their cell phones or sleeping on their desks.

I would always bring in a couple of books by African American authors that I hoped some of the students might be interested in, or I would make photocopies from the art history textbook, trying to entice them with short, digestible pieces of information. There were maybe three students, out of thirty, who eagerly devoured the materials I brought in, and they were the reason I came back every day. Those few kids and the fact that I wanted to fence kept me teaching.

Now that my fencing career was on an upward swing, I wanted to dedicate the majority of my time to training, but being an aspiring world-class athlete doesn't come with a paycheck, so I had to keep my teaching job. Between tournament fees, airplane tickets, hotel rooms, and food, the average cost to compete in one World Cup competition was around $2,000, and there were eight World Cups each season. What a disaster it would have been not to be able to compete because I couldn't afford it. So I continued to hustle, working at the school and picking up a second job coaching the fencing team at Columbia High School. Sometimes I wanted to tell my substitute-teaching students about my fencing goals, but I held back. The one time I'd started to talk about fencing, one of the boys interrupted me and said, "Wait, you build fences?" Everyone thought that was funny, and I didn't bother to correct him.

It was hard not to compare what I was witnessing every day in Newark with what I observed back in Maplewood, where I was coaching. Granted, coaching suburban kids in a sport that they enjoyed was completely different from teaching art history in a struggling inner-city high school, but the gap between the students was massive—and depressing. Students in Maplewood had nice desks and bathrooms with no graffiti. This wasn't just a case of black versus white, either. Most of the kids at Columbia were white, but they were still rambunctious and silly, and I had to repeat myself over and over again to get them to do what I asked on the strip. But they were eager to learn. They wanted my advice and directions. They didn't roll their eyes at me when I demanded more from them. I wished I knew how I could inspire my kids in Newark, to get that kind of hunger from them, but I didn't know where to begin. So I did my best and hoped that, by showing up, they knew I cared.

I tried to be the same kind of positive role model to my little sister. Faizah admitted she had initially resisted fencing because she really didn't want to stand in my shadow, but when she showed up at tryouts her freshman year at Columbia High, Coach Mustilli had discovered her talents as a fierce saber fencer. Now she was sixteen and dominating on the high school fencing circuit—better than I had ever done. She had an almost undefeated record and was frequently named the best female saber fencer in the state. Of course I didn't play favorites while I was coaching, but she really made me proud, and it was through fencing that Faizah and I morphed from sisters to best friends. Now I had someone to talk to who could understand my world. And she had someone who could guide her in the sport.

Even though I had broken through so many color barriers while I was in high school, six years later my little sister was still facing pushback and discrimination as a successful black female fencer and hijabi. Whether it was comments from parents or being given a hard time by coaches or referees, Faizah had to deal with all of it.

"Ibtihaj, they say I can't fence because of my hijab!" Faizah came up to me breathless, her large brown eyes wide with emotion. She was supposed to fence in ten minutes, but a referee was questioning her paperwork. We were at the Santelli Tournament, the largest high school fencing competition in the nation, where all of the state's teams competed for the championship title.

"What's going on?" I asked. "I already filed the paperwork for your hijab." Every time Faizah fenced, we had to have official paperwork from the New Jersey Board of Education stating that her hijab was for religious reasons. I always made sure to submit Faizah's paperwork early, at the start of the season. There must have been some mistake.

"They said they don't have my paperwork, and if they don't have it, I can't fence," she said again, panic creeping into her voice.

"Don't worry, Faizah. Go over to your strip and just get ready to fence. I'll take care of it." I meant it. After witnessing this type of incident before, I always came prepared. I had an extra copy of Faizah's paperwork in my bag, so I grabbed it and tracked down the referee in question.

"My athlete says you don't have her paperwork."

The man, who looked to be in his early fifties, took the papers I handed over and put on his glasses before studying them. Even though it was a standard letter of only about ten lines, he took an extraordinary amount of time going over it. Finally, fearing he was going to make

Faizah miss her bout, I spoke up. "Is everything okay? It's the same letter we've been using for the last three and half years without any problems."

Finally the referee looked up at me. He didn't smile. "Okay, she's good. But make sure you get this stuff in before we start next time. We need to have it early."

I wanted to argue, but I held my tongue. I didn't want any confrontation to affect Faizah's outcome on the strip. Since saber fencing is so subjective—the referee ultimately decides every contested point—I didn't want to give him any reason not to award points to my sister. So I just smiled, said thank you, and ran over to tell Faizah that everything was okay.

"Thank you *so* much," she said, the worry practically melting off her face.

"Don't thank me," I told her, giving her a quick pat on the back. "Just win."

And of course, she did.

When I look back at the hectic schedule I was leading—teaching, coaching, and training—it's a wonder I didn't burn out. But I was on a winning streak of my own, and the better my results, the harder I wanted to work.

I looked at every competition as an opportunity for the unmatched feeling of exhilaration I got when I scored the perfect touch. And Akhi was right there with me, continuing to work with me at the foundation every day, fine-tuning my technique and pushing me harder than ever.

Our next strategy was to see if I could win big on the world stage. We both had our sights on the upcoming World Cup and a grand prix in Tunisia, a Muslim country on the North African coast. My London showing earlier in the season had been disappointing, but the last six months of training had made a difference. I was getting stronger and gaining confidence in my own abilities.

Winning at a grand prix gives you more points than you get at a World Cup, so it is a great opportunity to help your world ranking. My national ranking was steadily climbing, but I had yet to really break through on the international World Cup circuit. I'd become more consistent in winning my pool matches and a few direct elimination bouts, but there was nothing to brag about. The Tunisia Grand Prix felt like my unofficial debut. If I could remain consistent, advance to the second day of competition, and win my first few direct elimination bouts, I'd have my first major international result.

Unlike on my trip to London with Candace, this time I traveled with Akhi, and I wasn't nervous. I was excited. Akhi kept reminding me that believing in myself and being in the right head space when stepping onto that strip was just as important as being in prime physical shape. "You can do this" looped through my mind repeatedly, serving as a mantra for anything that came next. It helped that we were competing in a Muslim country, surrounded by people who looked like me, so I didn't have to worry about how I would be received.

It was a fifteen-hour journey, including a three-hour layover in Istanbul, but when we landed in Tunis and got to the hotel, Akhi insisted that I stay awake. "You have to try to acclimate as soon as possible to the time difference so you can be at your best when you compete," he said.

While stifling a yawn, I replied, "Okay."

Akhi didn't look convinced. "Look, put your stuff in your room and meet me in the hotel lobby in fifteen minutes." I promised I would, and after getting my key to my room, I headed to the elevators. Fifteen minutes later I was showered, changed, and back in the lobby. I quickly spotted Akhi in his navy-blue Team USA warm-up, standing near the water fountain. I walked over to him.

He looked at me and smiled. "Well, you look much more awake. Are you ready?"

"Ready for what?" I said. "Where are we going?"

"We're going to go check out our surroundings. This is going to be your home for the next four days, and you need to know how to get around, where to go for food and water, and how to get to the venue. We don't wait to do those things on the day of the competition."

"Makes sense," I said.

"Of course it does, that's why I'm the coach," Akhi said with a knowing grin. "Let's go."

And with that, I followed my coach out of the hotel into the dry heat of Tunis. We spent the day wandering around the neighborhood, finding restaurants and cafés where we could eat for an affordable price. We caught a cab to the fencing venue so that on game day I would be familiar with the layout. And the last stop on our tour was a small market where Akhi had me buy a package of plain crackers, bottled water, almonds, and two bananas. When I showed off a little and used my basic Arabic to thank the storekeeper, Akhi raised one of his bushy eyebrows.

"Impressive. I know who to call if I'm in a pinch here."

"I won't be that helpful because I have the Arabic vocabulary of a second grader," I admitted.

Akhi laughed as we headed toward the hotel. When we got back, I thanked him for hanging out with me.

"Hey, I may be new at this as a coach, but after traveling so much as an athlete, I have learned what to do when I land someplace new for a competition," Akhi said. "This is my routine wherever I go. And it should be yours, too."

I nodded. "Okay. Got it."

Even though it was only 7:00 PM, we both said good night. I had now officially been awake for twenty-seven hours, and I was dying to go to sleep. As I rode up the elevator, I realized how nice it had been to stroll around a Muslim country in my hijab and receive nothing more than warm smiles of recognition from the people on the street. Tunisia reminded me so much of Morocco, and walking around all day with Akhi, I never once felt like I was different. With a clear mind and a happy heart, I could now fall asleep thinking about one thing—winning.

Like the majority of the other fencers registered in the competition, I began the first day of the grand prix warming up for pools. Almost two hundred athletes had to be narrowed down to forty-eight. Those forty-eight lucky enough to advance to the second day of competition would join the top sixteen fencers in the world for the direct elimination bracket of sixty-four. Before I went off for my first bout, Akhi reminded me to be confident and remember the game plan, and that's exactly what I did. Three hours later Akhi applauded me for going undefeated in the pool round, winning all six of my bouts, and directly advancing on to the second day of competition.

I wasn't just a little excited. I was over the moon! At the end of the first day I'd already performed better than

I had in London. Unfortunately, the tough part was yet to come: advancing through the bracket of sixty-four. But I decided that whatever happened on day two of the grand prix, I would be ready.

The following morning I rose early, even before the sun, to perform my morning prayers in my hotel room. I took an extra moment to thank Allah for allowing me to reach this stage and for helping me find the strength and courage to win the matches that lay ahead of me. As I sat on the floor near the hotel window, I thought about my mother, who had agreed to pay for half of my plane ticket and hotel fees because fencing ate up everything I earned.

Having the financial and emotional support of my parents made me thankful and often helped me find purpose in my journey. I knew it wasn't easy for them—for reasons bigger than money. In fact, Faizah had recently confided in me that some family friends were giving my parents a hard time because of my traveling schedule.

"Mommy said some of the sisters at the *masjid* were asking about you," Faizah told me.

"What did they say?" I asked, trying to keep my voice neutral so I wouldn't show my little sister that I actually cared.

"They told Mommy that they were surprised she let you travel all over the world by yourself. And they said you should be traveling with your father or brother at least. They made it sound like Mommy and Abu were doing something wrong by letting you go to your competitions instead of focusing on a career and marriage prospects."

I shook my head. "Look, I don't need to justify to people how I interpret my faith. I'm a grown woman. I also don't expect people to understand my journey, and I'm not going to let their opinions cloud my vision."

The truth was that it *was* sometimes frustrating that I didn't always have the support of people around me. But I felt most guilty that my mother had to listen to that nonsense. My whole family had made sacrifices, and the last thing I wanted to do was cause anyone pain or embarrassment.

Back in the US, my mother and younger sisters met me at the airport with a bouquet of flowers and a single balloon that read SWEET 16. I was coming home from Tunis in triumph. For the first time ever, I had cracked the top sixteen and secured a twelfth-place finish. Just seeing my name nearing the top of list, with Akhi by my side, I'd felt so proud. We'd done this together. And now here was my family sharing in my joy.

More success was just around the corner for me. Because of my twelfth-place finish in Tunisia and my earlier gold-medal wins in the domestic tournaments, my national ranking had improved significantly. Some fencers keep close tabs on their ranking; they calculate their standing themselves even before the official rankings are announced. Sometimes they're a little off, but for the most part they know exactly where they rank at all times. I'm a naturally competitive person, but I wasn't so obsessive that I had to know what my ranking was going to be every single second of every single day. That would have been an added layer of pressure and stress I didn't need. So when the final standings went up, I found out with everyone else. That's why, when the news broke that I had qualified for my first US world championship team, I was shocked. It was official; I was now one of the top four women's saber fencers in the entire United States, earning me a spot on my first national team. At age twenty-four, after working with my new coach for just a year, with the odds stacked against me, I had finally made it. Just like Coach Mustilli had predicted!

— CHAPTER —
11
Never Give Up

We are the ones we've been waiting for. We are the change that we seek.

—President Barack Obama

The first time I walked into the foundation after the announcement had been made, people stopped what they were doing. Suddenly the space erupted in applause, with everyone shouting their congratulations. I laughed and let the tears slide down my cheeks without even bothering to wipe them away. I had made my first national team and would be representing the United States of America at the Fencing World Championships. Since I was a member of the team, the majority of my competition expenses, like airfare, food, and hotel, would be covered. I could now officially say that I had a career in fencing. Though part of me felt sad about leaving my art history students behind, I could now quit teaching and focus on training full-time.

Technically, I wouldn't be earning a salary; instead I received a training stipend from USA Fencing, the official organizing body of fencing in the United States. My stipend was a predetermined amount of money to defray the cost of training expenses. Since I lived with my parents, the money—which turned out to be almost the same amount as my teaching salary—would be just enough to subsidize the costs of my personal trainer, gym membership, massage therapist, fencing equipment, and countless other training expenses.

There aren't many people who can call themselves professional fencers. There's not a league like the WNBA, and sponsorships are few and far between. But in order to qualify for an Olympic team, you have to commit full-time. Even on the world championship team there wouldn't be much time outside of training, travel, and competition for much else. So while I decided to keep coaching the team at Columbia High School because I had a close bond with the kids and loved them (and the extra money was great!), I realized that I might have to quit that at some point, too.

Standing in the foundation with my fencing family

applauding only made the moment more real. After all my hard work trying to make it, this was the first time since graduating from college that I felt like I had finally achieved something meaningful. I was no longer chasing rainbows; I was looking at my pot of gold, and everyone at the foundation had witnessed my fight.

They also knew I'd taken us one step closer to diversifying fencing. Our unwritten foundation motto was "When one wins, we all win," so Peter came over and gave me a big hug. He then asked for the attention of all 150 kids, adult students, and coaches on the floor.

"I want everyone here to take a look at Ibtihaj Muhammad. She has just qualified for the United States women's saber team and will represent our country at the world championships." Peter paused and looked at me. "Did you ever give up, Ibtihaj?"

Awkwardly, I managed to squeak out, "No."

"That's right," Peter said. "She never gave up, and neither can you if you want to be successful. In fencing and in life. If your coach is telling you that your parry isn't right, don't give up, fix it. If you keep falling short in your attack, don't give up, keep trying until you land that attack with your eyes closed and one hand tied behind your back. And most of all, don't you ever give up because someone tries to tell you that you don't belong because you don't look the part. Ibtihaj didn't listen to any of that non-sense, and she stands here in front of you triumphant."

The whole room erupted in applause again, and a small group turned to congratulate Akhi, too. After all, he'd never given up on *me*! There were a lot of young women who'd left the foundation over the years because they hadn't felt supported or encouraged. He'd done the opposite.

All of a sudden everyone started chanting his name. "Akhi! Akhi!" They wanted him to make a small speech. We locked eyes across the room, and he smiled. "I don't have time for speeches," he said with a grin. "Just because I helped Ibtihaj get onto the national team doesn't mean I'm done. Our work has just begun."

And with that pronouncement, Peter sent everyone back to training.

My spot on Team USA definitely carried with it a new level of respect, and I was no longer walking around with a giant question mark over my head. When I'd come back from Duke, I'd been treated like an afterthought, but now all the coaches at the foundation saw real potential in me. The upcoming 2012 Olympics were even being mentioned in my presence. But I couldn't let it get to my head. Now that I was going to wear red, white, and blue in competitions, I felt even more pressure to elevate my skills and become the best fencer I could.

Like gymnastics or track and field, fencing has both individual and team events. During competitions with Team
USA, the first two days are every woman for herself, and
depending on how the bracket is configured, two people
from the same country or team could face each other in
the direct elimination rounds. On the day of the team
event, we compete individually (since, of course, there's no
group fencing) but our scores come together as a team.
That kind of setup made for an interesting dynamic,
because it meant my teammates were one day my opponents and the next day my lifelines.

Qualifying for Team USA didn't mean I stopped
training with Akhi. There was a national coach for the
team, but most team members traveled to competitions
with their personal coaches as well. The competition season ran from January through October, with about ten
international competitions per season. Theoretically, we
were supposed to have at least one World Cup in each
zone of the world—the Americas, Africa, Europe, and
Asia—but the competitions were predominately held in
Europe, with a few in Asia. In between the World Cups
we also had four domestic competitions (North American Cups, or NACs), held in different cities around the

United States. Those competitions would occur in January, April, October, and December. Every season culminated with the world championships, unless it was an Olympic year.

I'd been following the careers of two of the team's fencers since graduating from college. These women had consistently been ranked in the top four and formed the base of the team, leaving the other two spots for wild cards like me. One was named Mariel Zagunis. The child of Olympic rowers, Mariel was the most decorated American fencer, male or female, and had been fencing since she was ten. She'd won individual gold medals at the 2004 and 2008 Olympics, and had been on the national team since 2000. Dagmara Wozniak, a Polish American immigrant, had been fencing since she was nine years old and had been the alternate on the women's saber team at the 2008 Olympics. Even though Mariel and Dagmara had been fencing far longer than I had, we were all around the same age. Mariel was twenty-four, like me, and Dagmara was twenty-one. The third member of the team when I joined in 2010 wasn't my friend Candace. She'd stopped fencing in order to enroll in law school. It was instead a woman named Daria Schneider. Daria was a strong fencer who had just missed a chance to compete in the 2008 Olympics, but who had done really well on the college circuit, for Columbia University. All told, my new teammates were an elite group of athletes who had been raised to become fencing champions. It was awe inspiring to be part of such a talented team, and I promised myself I'd prove worthy of my spot on the squad.

Our first competition as a team was the world championships in October. Akhi and I had been training overtime, and I felt as ready as I ever had to get on the strip. Because all four team members lived and trained in different parts of the country, we arrived in Paris separately. I was so excited to be at my first world championships representing the United States that I must have seemed like a happy puppy; eagerness radiated from every inch of my body. I was so looking forward to bonding with Mariel and Dagmara, too. These were women who, like me, understood the level of intensity and sacrifice required to reach athletic excellence. Though we lived separate lives in different places, we were all trying to find enough time in the day to eat, sleep, and drink fencing. We were on the same mission.

The national coach for the women's saber team was the highly respected Polish saber fencer Ed Korfanty. Ed had had an illustrious fencing career in his native Poland before immigrating to the United States and starting to coach in Portland, Oregon. Not only had he coached

Coach Mustilli's elder daughter when she was on the US women's saber team back in 2000, he was also Mariel's personal coach.

My sister Brandilyn and my mom came along with me. People say everything is better in Paris—the food, the architecture, the romance. I found even fencing belonged on that list. I had traveled to a handful of other countries to fence, but these world championships felt magical. The entire experience was like something out of a Disney movie. The competition took place at the historic Grand Palais, an exhibition hall normally reserved for art and cultural exhibits. The grandeur of the ornate glass structure made me think it must have at one point been a playground for royalty. I was used to fencing in convention centers or sports arenas, but this was a whole different level of spectacular.

Mom, Brandilyn, and I toured the Grand Palais the night before the competition. Stepping foot in the historic glass palace with vaulted ceilings that offered clear views of the dark night sky, we were in awe, drinking it all in. Not a single word passed between us. And then I broke the silence.

"I am going to *love* fencing in here. It's like a fairy tale."

"You are so corny," Brandilyn joked. "But this place *is* gorgeous."

Mom just shook her head, too overwhelmed to put into words what she was feeling. Finally she smiled and said, "Truly a blessing from Allah."

The next morning, wearing my national team warm-up, I headed over to the venue early, while my mom and Brandilyn went off to sightsee. Right before I reached the Grand Palais, a young Muslim girl in hijab stopped me.

"Excuse me," she said with a thick French accent. "Can I have your autograph?"

I gave her a funny look. "You want *my* autograph?"

"Because you are the famous American fencer wearing hijab. We have read about you in the newspaper. I want your autograph because I look up to you. I want to be an athlete like you."

I had no idea that the few small articles that had been written about me back home had made it all the way to France!

I wanted to tell the girl that I wasn't a celebrity, but I signed her paper and wished her good luck. She thanked me profusely and ran off. Before I could process the interaction, another hijabi girl and her mother approached me, and I signed autographs for them, too.

This was a totally new experience for me, and I felt kind of weird getting extra attention because people hadn't seen a Muslim woman fence before. But after getting over the initial shock of being considered special, I thought it was kind of cool. I'd never thought of wearing hijab as being anything extraordinary—it was just something I did. It was other people who defined it as exotic or dangerous. I hadn't thought of myself as a role model, but that day I realized I could provide a vision of hope for kids.

When it came time to fence my first bout, the faces of the young women who'd asked for my autograph that morning flashed before me. As I placed my mask over my head, I blocked out the noise of the audience, and I fenced for young Ibtihaj and for every young Muslim girl I'd ever met. *I can win for all of us*, I told myself.

And as I wielded my saber against one opponent after another, I felt the strength in my whole body respond to my demands. I smiled behind my mask as I locked out opponent after opponent. I felt invincible on the strip, and for a long time I was. I kept winning, fighting my way to a chance at the final, before losing 14–5 to 2008 Olympic champion Olena Khomrova. I left the tournament with a fourteenth-place finish, and I was ecstatic. It was my highest finish ever in a competition that big and important.

On the flight back I melted into my seat, exhausted and exhilarated at the same time. It had been the hardest tournament of my life, but I'd never given up. In the end, I'd more or less proven that I was the fourteenth-best women's saber fencer in the world—and my career was just getting started. Best of all, I'd shared it with two of the most important people in my life: Mom and Brandilyn.

During my first year on the national team, I was a work-horse who showed no mercy on the strip, but I was a lamb among my teammates, trying my best to fit in. Even though we all maintained our own individual training schedules back at home, we were often required to attend training camps, so I figured I'd have plenty of opportunities to form friendships.

Unfortunately, that didn't happen—with my teammates or our coach.

One time, at a training camp during the beginning of the season, Ed instructed us to free fence, and I was paired with an up-and-coming fencer named Melanie.

"Can we stop for a minute?" Melanie huffed, taking her mask off.

I glanced at the clock on the wall and realized we'd been fencing awhile without any specific instruction or direction from Ed. I turned around and scanned the massive gym, looking for him, and noticed him in a huddle with Dagmara on the other side of the room. From where I stood, it looked like they were talking tactics.

"Hold on, Melanie," I said. "Let me go see what Ed wants us to do."

I jogged across the gymnasium, and as I got closer to the two of them, I stopped running and hovered at a respectable distance. I didn't want to barge in on their conversation. I stood there for a minute but soon realized that Ed wasn't speaking to Dagmara in English. I strained my ears and listened for any familiar-sounding words, and when I could hear none, I assumed it was his native Polish. I stood there for a minute longer, then finally cleared my throat, even though I figured they must have noticed me by then.

"Excuse me," I said. "Melanie and I were wondering if you wanted us to rotate partners."

"Ibti," Ed said, struggling to pronounce even my shortened nickname correctly, "please keep working on what I told you. I'll let you know when it's time to stop. Don't be so quick to give up. Don't be lazy."

I pressed down on my lips, sealing my mouth shut. I didn't want to say something I might regret. But me, lazy? Did this man not understand that all I knew was hard work? That in the dictionary under "work ethic" there's a picture of me? The insult—especially in front of my teammates—burned inside me. I clenched my teeth and turned to head back to Melanie. As I walked away, the coach said something in Polish, and he and Dagmara shared a laugh.

Getting off to a rocky start with the team didn't sit well with me, and in fact, I was shocked. I'd always been so comfortable and happy in the cafeteria at Columbia High or at the foundation, being around people who lived and breathed fencing like me. Didn't this shared passion automatically make us close? Apparently not.

But I refused to let this snub distract me from my purpose of becoming one of the world's best fencers. And I wasn't going to let it deter me from continuously trying to break the ice between my teammates and myself. It wasn't easy, since I was new to the team, but I did my best to assimilate into team culture, and I tried to be super friendly, with a smile on my face all the time. When we were on the road, I tried to initiate team dinners and arrange group outings. I was silent during disagreements and would compliment my teammates to show them I appreciated their skill on the strip. But my efforts to make friends were useless. My dinner suggestions were often turned down, as were my invitations to watch movies in our hotel rooms or sightsee when we arrived in a new city.

"Is there any plan to go out for a team dinner?" I asked the team manager, Cathy, once after practice. We were at a World Cup competition, and I had heard some talk of going out to a restaurant instead of eating at the hotel.

"No, not this time, Ibtihaj," Cathy told me. "You should probably just order in and be ready for the competition tomorrow."

I went back to my room, deflated. All the travel was beginning to weigh on me. I was lonely. Akhi hadn't been able to make it to this tournament, so I felt homesick, but I consoled myself with the knowledge that I'd have more time to sleep and prepare for tomorrow's competition.

The next morning when I boarded the bus to head over to the venue, I sat next to Daria.

"What did you do for dinner last night?" I asked. "I ordered from the restaurant in the hotel, and it was really good."

Daria turned to Mariel before answering. "Oh, we all went to this restaurant near the hotel."

"We tried to call your room but got no answer," Dagmara jumped in.

"That's strange," I said, wrinkling up my forehead. "My phone never rang, and I don't show any missed calls."

Dagmara shrugged. "I don't know who made the call, but I know someone did. Anyway, you didn't really miss anything. The food wasn't that good."

I turned to Cathy, who also happened to be Mariel's mother. "You told me there was no team dinner," I said.

Never taking her eyes from the pages of her magazine, Cathy responded, "Ibtihaj, it was nothing official. If it had been, I would have told you."

"Right," I said doubtfully. I was hurt. They clearly hadn't invited me on purpose. I leaned my head against the window and closed my eyes. I tried to sleep, willing the ride to be over as soon as possible.

I spent the rest of my first year on the national team progressing as an athlete as I worked to climb the rankings, but socially my efforts to blend with my teammates consistently failed. I realized the girls had known one another longer, but I wondered if their behavior was intentional. They would routinely watch movies together in one of their hotel rooms but never invite me. When they made plans for dinner, I never got a call to tag along. I was sometimes even left off of e-mail chains. Because we were a team of only four, being the one person left out when the other three got together was extra hurtful.

My mother would try to console me, telling me, "Ibtihaj, when you have three sisters, you have all of the girlfriends you need. You don't need them to be your friends."

I knew my mom was right. I didn't *need* them to be my friends, but spending so much time on the road, away from family and friends, was hard enough, without the pain of feeling like "the other."

In general, it seemed my teammates and the coaching staff didn't understand who I was as a fencer. Some thought of my qualifying for the national team as a stroke of luck and attributed my wins to brute strength and blind speed. Like so many other black athletes, I was being pigeonholed as strong but not smart. That stereotype was incredibly frustrating, not to mention disheartening. Despite my success on the strip, I was feeling increasingly unhappy, and I wanted so badly to understand what I had done to make my teammates and the coaching staff treat me so coldly. Though I struggled for months to come up with a reason why, I finally arrived at the conclusion that the women's saber team was not ready for change. These women saw me as someone so different, almost a different species, whom they couldn't relate to and who had arrived uninvited. I reflected a lot on my experiences of exclusion, and I realized that the more success I'd had, the harsher the treatment from teammates and coaches had been.

I looked for other friends when I was on the road,

though. Rather than hanging out in my hotel room alone, I started to spend time with fencers from other countries, and I always found any number of people willing and eager to share a meal or go sightseeing. It was often a struggle to feel like an outsider on my own team, but I made up my mind early on that I wasn't going to let it affect my goals. And my new goal was to make it to the 2012 Olympics in London.

— CHAPTER —
12

Dream Big

We realize the importance of our voices only when we are silenced.

—Malala Yousafzai

Because I was an underdog who'd been on the team for only one season, and because no one except Coach Mustilli had ever even mentioned my name in the same breath as the Olympics, I didn't tell anyone about my wish. I knew Mariel and Dagmara were favorites to qualify, but I just kept asking myself, *Why not me, too?* When I fenced with Mariel and Dagmara, they were formidable opponents, but they didn't have anything that I didn't have. What I lacked in experience, I made up for with heart and determination. My time would come.

But I failed first. It wasn't a huge loss, and to some it

might have seemed like I had just had an off day, but after a season on the domestic circuit where I was always on the medal podium, I didn't make the top sixteen in one tournament. I took it hard, and for the first time in a long time, when my last match was over, I cried.

Back in my hotel room, I called my sister Faizah. She had graduated from high school and was now attending Rutgers University along with my sister Asiya. Faizah had started competing on the national and international circuits, so she understood how devastating a loss could feel.

"It was awful, Faizah," I said as I felt the tears forming again. "I haven't lost like that in a long time."

"What was the score?"

"Fifteen to seven."

"That's not so bad," Faizah cooed into the phone. "And this was just one tournament. You've won so many more than you've lost."

"But this whole tournament I felt off. And it didn't help that Ed yelled at me afterward."

Faizah sighed. "Ignore him. He doesn't care about you or how you do. If he doesn't say anything positive to you when you win, then he doesn't get to say anything to you when you have a bad day. Period."

My little sister was so wise, and she knew me better than anyone else. She had become my closest confidante, and I depended on her more and more to help me ride through the ups and downs of being a member of the US team. When I hung up the phone, I felt a million times better.

The tournament was going to start in one hour. I was going through the motions of my warm-up, but inside I was fighting the urge to go curl up in a corner somewhere and take a nap. The thing was, I'd gotten plenty of rest on the flight over from the States and had had a good night's sleep. I knew I wasn't sleep deprived, yet fatigue was over-whelming me.

I went to the bathroom and splashed water on my face. I forced myself into a longer warm-up routine than nor-mal, but I couldn't shake the exhaustion. In fact, I had this strange sensation like someone was pouring warm water over me, starting from my head all the way down to the tips of my toes. I glanced up at the clock and real-ized I had only thirty more minutes before my first bout, so somehow I had to push through this feeling and get on the strip.

This same thing had been happening to me for the last couple of competitions, and I knew that once I started fencing, the fatigue would fade just as swiftly as it had come. But as soon as the bout was over, another tidal wave of exhaustion would hit me. Since saber is all about speed and explosive energy, feeling slow before every competition was a big concern. And because I didn't know if the problem was physical or mental, I wasn't sure where to turn for help.

Sometimes the universe conspires to help those in need. This was one of those occasions. While I was in the midst of another bout of fatigue, the US Olympic Committee assigned us an official team psychologist, Jamie Harshaw. I'm not sure if this was something they always did, but regardless, the timing could not have been better. Jamie met with each team member individually for a basic psychological evaluation and checkup, and when it was my turn, I told her about my issue.

"Maybe what you're experiencing is anxiety manifesting itself as fatigue," she said calmly. "Other people hyperventilate or feel faint when they're having a panic attack, but yours may be the opposite."

Jamie's assessment made complete sense. Perhaps my anxiety stemmed from a fear of total failure, like I'd have to quit fencing and go back to the Dollar Store. Or maybe I was worried that I wouldn't meet my own high expectations, such as winning an Olympic medal. But I quickly realized I had been suffering from performance anxiety in the moments before competing, and now I had to learn how to manage those worries and fight some of the triggers.

Jamie and I met regularly, and she gave me exercises I could walk myself through to lessen the anxiety. With Jamie's help I learned different breathing techniques and ways to use guided imagery to help me. I would take fifteen minutes before I began my warm-up to focus on my breathing and my thoughts. I would tell myself, *I'm ready. I'm prepared. I'm strong. I'm a champion.* These mantras helped me visualize the future, to see myself winning, and stay away from replaying issues from previous competitions. Remembering past losses wasn't helpful, and those thoughts creeping into my head before competitions created anxiety. The truth was I *was* prepared for battle, and I had no reason to doubt my abilities.

Once I was able to manage my anxiety better, I returned my focus to the next big thing: making the 2012 Olympic team.

Despite my strange dance with anxiety, in the two years since I landed on the US national women's saber team, I had been doing more winning than losing. In 2011 I had qualified for my first Pan American Games, held in Guadalajara, Mexico, capturing the gold medal along with my teammates. We'd won two team medals at the Fencing World Championships, both bronze, one in 2011 in Catania, Italy, and the other in 2012 in Kiev, Ukraine. And I had won a few individual medals at World Cups throughout the season, helping both my domestic and my world rankings. In early 2012 I was ranked number two in the United States and thirteenth in the world. With those stats, my qualifying for an Olympic team was likely, and Akhi thought I could do it. My family believed I would, too, and even the media covered my story, saying I had a real shot.

But I didn't make the team.

Part of the setback was beyond my control. In 2012 there was no women's saber team event at the Olympics, only the individual event. That left only two possible slots for Americans in the individual competitions instead of the usual four. When the qualification year came to a close, I wasn't among the top two Americans selected to represent the United States, and that was that.

Even though I was disappointed, I wasn't entirely surprised. I hadn't had a strategy to qualify for the Games, other than to continue to train hard. But that hadn't been enough. Like Peter had told me, I'd needed to lay out a plan to help me get there, but I hadn't done that, and I hadn't had the coaching to help me.

Fortunately, failing to qualify for the team in 2012 sparked a flame. It helped me realize that I had come a long way, but the journey was just beginning. If I truly wanted to be in the next Olympics, I would have to make even more changes and sacrifices—not just for my own future success, but as a representative of African Americans and Muslims around the world.

There are about 6.5 million Muslims in America, living in every state and employed in thousands of different professions. There are Muslim student groups at almost every college and university in the country. Throughout the year thousands of Muslims attend regional and national conventions in North America, and there's even an annual Muslim Family Day at Six Flags amusement parks.

It was within this Muslim community that I gained my first level of celebrity status as an athlete. This made sense to me because the Muslim community in the United States was still relatively small. When it came to professional female athletes who wore hijab, I was one in a group of one. So I quickly became a public figure, regularly traveling to speak about my experiences as a minority member of Team USA. From campus visits to conference keynotes, I got invitations from all across the United States.

Mistakenly, people in the Muslim community often referred to me as "the Olympic fencer." I knew it was an honest mistake, but because I had failed to qualify, it hurt every time I had to correct someone and say, "Sorry, I'm not an Olympian." I didn't want anyone to feel bad for me, because I didn't feel sorry for myself. I believed in Allah's plan for me and that the Olympic Games weren't meant for me yet. I had moved on and had my eyes set on the future.

One day not long after the London 2012 Summer Games ended, I was out shopping with my friend Habiba. This particular store we were in had a pretty big selection of modest formal dresses, and we wondered if one or two would be right for some of the special events and speeches I had coming up. As a professional athlete who spent the majority of her time in sweatpants and sneakers, I jumped at any opportunity to dress up. That was another stereotype I was trying to break—that fashion and sports are mutually exclusive. I was an athlete *and* I loved dressing up. I wore eyeliner most days, even when I fenced, and didn't care how anyone felt about it.

Before I could find a dress I wanted to try on, I heard a voice call out.

"Excuse me, are you Ibtihaj Muhammad? The Olympic fencer?"

A young girl I'd never met stood in front of me, extending a piece of paper and a pencil. She was wearing blue jeans, a pink checkered shirt, and a blue hijab. I guessed she was probably eleven or twelve years old. I started to respond, but Habiba jumped in to answer for me.

"Actually, she's not an Olympian."

I turned my head and glared at Habiba.

"Can I still have your autograph?" the little girl said, not noticing my discomfort.

"Oh, of course," I said, taking the paper from her hand and scribbling my name and some kind words.

"Thank you," she said, and rewarded me with a huge smile. "I want to be just like you when I grow up. Except I don't want to fence. I'm going to the Olympics to run track."

I smiled, wishing her the best of luck, and told her never to give up on her dreams. It was such an endearing moment, but I was a little annoyed at Habiba. Sure, she'd only told the truth—I *wasn't* an Olympian—but the reality was, it hurt to hear someone else revealing that painful fact so plainly.

"Let's go, Habiba," I said as I headed for the department store exit. "I'm going to order a dress online."

Luckily, Habiba didn't try to change my mind. She sensed I was annoyed. We said our good-byes, and I hopped in my car and headed back home.

While I was driving, I replayed the scene in the store and the visceral reaction I'd had in my gut. When Habiba announced that I wasn't an Olympian, it reminded me of all the people who hadn't believed in me—because I was black, because I was a woman, because I was Muslim, or because I was too old. I gripped the steering wheel tighter and forced myself to breathe calmly, but I couldn't tamp down the emotions brewing inside of me. That little girl from the department store deserved a role model. She deserved to see someone who looked like her in sports, on a major stage. When I'd started on this journey, I'd always told myself that I wanted to see how far fencing could take me, and now I realized that the journey was bigger than me. My success would mean so much to so many people. It was in that moment in my car, heading south on the turnpike, that I decided I was going to make the Olympic team if it was the last thing I ever did. Missing 2012 wasn't the end for me. I didn't care that it would be four years of grind. I didn't care how old I would be. I was going to be on the US Olympic team in the 2016 Summer Games. There was no other option.

— CHAPTER —
13

Build a Team

To be a champ you have to believe in yourself when no one else will.

—Sugar Ray Robinson

I knew everything in my training regimen had to be fine-tuned to get me where I wanted to be. I knew I needed to find people who could help me make the Olympics, so I started building a team of trainers and mentors who could help me formulate a plan, a training schedule, and a mind-set that would take me to the top. The individuals I was looking for needed to be smart and trustworthy, to have positive energy and a track record of excellence.

Unfortunately, I realized that Akhi might not be a part of that group for much longer. After he'd helped me reach the national team, he'd become a father, and now he was frequently absent from the foundation and my competitions. Family was hugely important to me, so I didn't resent him for spending time with his baby, but I missed him. Selfishly, I wanted him by my side all the time. But after all these years, I'd finally come to realize that depending on anyone other than myself was unrealistic. Ultimately, I was the one responsible for my own success, and if that meant I had to seek out another coach to help me, then that was exactly what I was going to do.

Keeth Smart was the first person I sought to be my mentor. Keeth had led the US men's saber team to a silver medal at the 2008 Olympic Games in Beijing and was arguably the best US male saber fencer of all time. He had since retired from competition, but he liked to come back to the Peter Westbrook Foundation—where he'd gotten his start—to mentor and teach the younger kids on Saturday mornings. He said it was his way of giving back after fencing had given him so much. From watching the way Keeth worked with the kids, it was easy to see he had a vast knowledge of fencing, and he would be able to help me master the tactics I needed. I started to pick Keeth's brain about his Olympic coaching, what kinds of things he'd focused on with his trainers, which drills I could incorporate into my practices to help with my speed, and more. Keeth had a demanding full-time job and wasn't even at the foundation that much, but he was kind enough to give me his cell number and make time to help me.

One of the most useful things Keeth did for me was to give me a list of seven simple exercises to do every day. He told me if I got to practice thirty minutes earlier than everyone else, four times a week, and plowed through these exercises, they would add up to make a difference. When I looked at the list, I was skeptical. How could doing jumps and lateral lunges, which seemed like nothing more than warm-ups, make me better?

"Don't cheat on these," Keeth said to me, noting the look of doubt on my face. "If you can commit to doing these drills, you will be building your craft exponentially and getting ahead of the competition. They'll help with your explosiveness and foot speed. Trust me."

I took the list and promised I'd start doing the exercises.

Keeth also asked me how much time I spent studying my competition. I told him about that first World Cup in London, where Candace and I had sat with our notebooks, watching the competition. I ran to my locker to grab my fencing journal—a simple black moleskin notebook with lined pages and furiously handwritten notes—and then showed it to Keeth. He flipped through the pages and saw the detailed descriptions I had of almost every woman I'd ever competed against over the years.

He was impressed. "This is really good. You can be the fastest woman on the strip, but it's important to fence every match smart. At the start of every competition, know who you're up against so you can strategize. You've put in too much time and energy to wing it. You can win sometimes with speed and strength, but if you want to be consistent and if you want to be the best, you have to be smart."

Sometimes Keeth would give me scenarios to try that he thought would work against certain fencers based on their style of fencing. I would write those down in my journal and refer to them often when I was on the road. My journal soon became my guide.

For years I had been working out at an all-women's gym in New Jersey, but I quickly realized I wasn't getting enough out of the facilities. I knew that I needed a gym that catered to athletes and understood their specific needs.

I soon found a gym a few towns over in Springfield, and once I started, it took me a while to find the right trainer.

Because of my faith, I debated whether or not I wanted to work with a male or female, but ultimately, I decided I'd settle on the best person for the job. When I met Jake, I knew he was the one. Initially, I didn't tell him I was on a national team, but I said I was a fencer and that I wanted to work on speed, strength, and agility. Jake was the type of trainer who, no matter what mood I was in or how much I might complain, wouldn't accept anything less than 100 percent in every workout. I soaked up his lighthearted toughness, but what I loved most was that he was totally dependable. Whether I needed or wanted to work out at a normal hour, at six o'clock in the morning, or at ten o'clock at night, Jake would be there.

After working with Jake, I realized that high-intensity strength training was the piece of the puzzle that I'd been missing. Now I could lunge farther and faster, I was stronger, and my speed picked up. With this small change in my workout regimen, I became a more well-balanced athlete. I diversified my training by incorporating reformer Pilates, kickboxing, and interval running, and my performance on the strip started showing that I was headed in the right direction.

I was stronger and fencing smarter, and my individual results began to climb, improving both my national and international rankings. The national team was impressive, too. In 2013 we won bronze medals at the World Cups in Italy, Turkey, and Belgium. And at the end of the season, we captured the bronze medal at the world championships in Budapest, Hungary.

While everything looked great on the outside, though, I was still waging a secret war with my teammates and coaching staff.

In March 2013 we attended a grand prix in Moscow, Russia. At that point the national team still consisted of Mariel, Dagmara, Daria, and myself. Although she wasn't officially on the team, a younger fencer named Eliza Stone was also traveling with us for the competition. Both Eliza and I fenced well on the first day of competition in Moscow. I advanced through my bracket, eliminating some heavy hitters on the world circuit, and Eliza and I tied for third place.

We were so happy we wanted to celebrate. There was a decent restaurant most teams frequented whenever they traveled to Moscow, and because it was late and the restaurant was next to the hotel, Eliza and I decided to go there.

It wasn't surprising that during my matches the rest of the US fencers hadn't bothered to cheer for me, especially since I'd knocked out Dagmara to get to the semifinals. But Eliza was disappointed that the team she hoped to join one day hadn't rooted her on as she made her run to the semifinals. I didn't want to dash her hopes by telling her all I'd witnessed on the team, so I downplayed their behavior.

"Don't worry about it," I said, trying to boost her confidence as we walked into the restaurant. "You fenced well today."

Eliza smiled. "I still can't believe it."

Then we stepped into the dimly lit restaurant, with its handful of mostly empty tables, and we both stopped in our tracks. There in the far corner sat the rest of the team: Mariel, Dagmara, and Daria.

We waited to see if our teammates would invite us to join them. They didn't. In fact, they didn't even wave.

A hostess appeared, greeted us in English, and led us to a table next to our teammates. No sooner had we sat down than Mariel, Dagmara, and Daria abruptly stood up and left the restaurant without saying a word to us. I think Eliza was shocked. I know I was. Even after all those years, I couldn't understand why they acted like that toward me—and now toward Eliza.

"What was that about?" Eliza asked, staring at their half-eaten dinners still on the table.

I shrugged. "I honestly do not know."

Eliza didn't look as if my answer satisfied her. She

clearly wanted to know more, but we agreed not to talk about them. I wouldn't let them ruin my evening. And I didn't want to color Eliza's opinions about her potential future teammates. So instead we ate and celebrated our success on the strip.

Despite the poor introduction to the team dynamic, Eliza continued her quest to make the national team, and she replaced Daria as the newest member. I was so excited to be teammates with Eliza; I finally had a shoulder to lean on through what had been a terribly lonely experience. Unfortunately for Eliza, though, sticking with me meant being iced out by Mariel and Dagmara, and that made me feel awful.

One year we trained in Poland before the world championships, and the camp happened to fall during Ramadan. Because it was summer and the days that far north were long, I was fasting for eighteen to nineteen hours a day. I would go to the cafeteria during dinner, pack my food into a container, and then eat in my room once the sun set around 11:00 PM. At 4:00 in the morning, when the sun was about to rise again, I would eat before starting the fast all over. Unfortunately, the coaching staff and my teammates didn't appreciate why I was fasting or make any attempts to understand the reasons it was important to me. The truth was that fasting allowed me to reflect on

Allah and his mercy. It was central to my spiritual growth and connection to my faith.

Ed continued to push me without pause. If I took a break or had a hard time catching my breath, he told me I was being lazy. I wouldn't say much; I'd just get back on the strip and do my best. I wasn't looking to force religion on anyone, but a tiny bit of understanding could have gone a long way. His attitude toward me and fasting felt like, *I don't understand why you would choose to kill yourself.*

By this point my fencing career on Team USA had become a mental game. I had to find ways to block out all the distractions in order to fully focus on the goal ahead of me. There was an art to it, and it was something that, by the grace of Allah, I was eventually able to figure out. But not before I spent dozens of hours in tears around people who made me feel inferior and devalued.

"Ibtihaj!" my mother shouted one day in a crowded café in Maplewood. "Are you even listening to me?"

"Sorry, Mommy, what did you say?" I responded. It was that rare Sunday afternoon that I wasn't traveling for a competition.

"What I said," my mother repeated in a more soothing

tone, "is that I'm worried about you. You're killing your-self at the gym and at the foundation, and you come home from these competitions so upset."

I could feel a wall of tears gather behind my eyelids. My mother's concern was almost too much to bear because it meant I wasn't hiding my anguish very well. I was miser-able much of the time. I was in physical pain after almost every workout. Sometimes I couldn't sleep because I was so worried that I hadn't trained hard enough. Plus, I had to spend days and weeks with teammates and a coaching staff who didn't like me. Expending that kind of energy day in and day out was mentally and emotionally exhaust-ing, and now my mother could see it on my face.

I pulled in a deep breath of air and released it slowly. "I'm okay, Mommy."

"No, you're not," my mother said, and took a big gulp of her coffee. "I'm your mother and I think I know when my child is not okay."

I placed my hand over my mother's and gave it a squeeze. "I said I was going to do this, and I am not going to quit now because things are hard."

Now my mother looked like she was going to cry. Now it was her turn to breathe deep.

"Ibtihaj," she started, "you have always known what you wanted to do and no one could stop you once you made your mind up, so I'm not going to try. But I want you to understand that no one will think any of less of you if you decide to move on."

"I know," I said to my mom, but inside I was worrying that, even if I didn't disappoint my family, I'd still let down other people. I had made a promise to myself to make the Olympic team, and I had promised all the little girls who looked like me that I was going to go all the way. If I gave up now, how would I face them? How would I face myself? But to my mother I just said, "I promise you, Mom, that if it ever gets to be too much, I'll stop. But I'm not there yet."

I wasn't just trying to make my mother feel good. I wanted her to trust me, because I couldn't survive my journey to the Olympics without her. She was the center of my support team, along with Faizah. Now that my little sister was fencing more regularly, we often traveled together to the same competitions—even fencing against each other at tournaments. Things were so much better with her around. She witnessed firsthand some of the outlandish treatment I received at the hands of my team-mates, and someone else seeing it proved I wasn't crazy.

"I can't believe they 'forgot' to tell you about team practice," Faizah said to me one night before a tournament.

Somehow no one had thought it was important to tell me the time of a mandatory team practice Ed had scheduled. Then I was chastised when I arrived one hour late. This type of "accident" had become so common that I hardly blinked. I had gotten so used to being treated like a second-class citizen that these slights didn't even phase me anymore. But Faizah was incensed.

"I think they're just jealous because you're doing so well," she fumed.

"Maybe. I just can't give them any more of my energy by worrying about their issues." After three years on the team, I had finally gotten to the point where I refused to give it any more attention. Then I added, "Just having you here with me is enough. I want you to maintain your focus on winning as well. Don't let these people distract you from that."

"Is that how you handle all of this?" Faizah asked, her forehead wrinkled up in concern.

"Yeah," I said. I needed to give her the strength that no one had given me. "If it happens to you, put it aside so you can focus on the sport."

I had the impression that my little sister had appointed herself my protector on the fencing circuit. Sometimes it was just a look she shot me across the room, or there were times when she'd give me a high five to congratulate me on a bout well fought. Sometimes it felt like *she* was the older sister.

I often found myself without a personal coach in my corner, but I almost always had my own little cheering squad with Mom and Faizah. Though they didn't carry the same weight as a coach in the coach's box, they soothed my soul and buoyed my spirits to no end. I thanked Allah for having them in my life.

In 2013, toward the end of the season, we were at a World Cup in Bologna, Italy. I had one of my toughest brackets ever, against some of the best fencers in the world. These were the women that I'd been admiring since I started fencing, women whose bouts I studied on video replay as part of my training, like the Russian fencer Sofiya Velikaya. She had several world championship titles and an Olympic medal to her name. To me, she was like the Serena Williams of women's saber—and I had her in my bracket!

As I put on my mask and faced her, my last thought was, *I want to fence like her.* I wanted to be strong and confident in my actions, and that was exactly what I did, beating one of the best fencers in the world, by a score of 15–10. I had toppled one of the greatest, and I felt invincible all day. I made it all the way to the semifinals, which meant I was going home with a medal. The question was, what color it would be?

The semifinal match did not start out well. I was losing miserably, 13–4, but then something clicked inside of me. I found an awareness that if I could beat Velikaya, then I could beat anyone. My body caught up with my mind, and I rallied back on the strip to win the match against Ilaria Bianco, from Italy, 15–14. I ended up taking second place that day in Bologna, earning my first individual medal at a World Cup.

When I stood on that medal stand, I was so proud of myself that nothing could contain my happiness. But from the medal stand I could see my teammates, and not one of them was cheering. That's the moment I realized I really was out there on my own. We were individuals first, a team second, and I would be smart to always remember that.

Me at six months old in seven-year-old Brandilyn's lap with two-year-old Qareeb, all dressed to go to the circus.

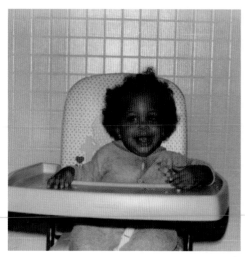

Sitting in my high chair, waiting for dinner.

At eighteen months old.

All smiles for Qareeb's pre-K graduation and my preschool moving-on celebration.

Having fun in the backyard as a six-year-old, with Qareeb and baby Faizah.

Abu, Qareeb, and me enjoying the warm weather while vacationing in Orlando, Florida, in 1993.

In Budapest, Hungary, with my mom in 2013 for the Fencing World Championships.

My teammates and me in Budapest, excited to capture the bronze medal at the world championship.

At the World Cup in Chicago, Illinois, gearing up with Team USA as we face Hungary.

After capturing the bronze medal at the 2014 Moscow Grand Prix in Russia.

Faizah makes her first final at a World Cup in Antalya, Turkey, in March 2014.

With one of my best friends, Paola Pliego, waiting for the next round of matches to begin in Panama City, Panama.

During the team event at the 2016 Olympic Games in Rio de Janeiro, Brazil, I face off against Sofya Velikaya of Russia.

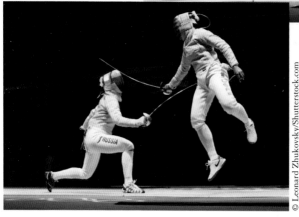

Celebrating a victory after a match in Rio!

On the podium at the Olympics, embracing one of the most surreal moments of my life.

My family taking in the sights during the Olympics in Rio. From left to right: Adam (Faizah's husband), Faizah, Qareeb and his son Zayd, Mommy, Abu, Asiya, family friend Joi, Qareeb's wife Denise, and best friend Isis.

A surprise party hosted by my family after my return from Rio. From left to right: Asiya, Faizah's sister-in-law Hannah, me, and Faizah.

Attending the 2017 TIME 100 Gala at Frederick P. Rose Hall in New York City.

The first Louella trunk show. From left to right: me, Faizah, Qareeb, and Asiya.

Posing in one of my favorite Louella by Ibtihaj Muhammad styles.

A quick selfie with Faizah at the Global Village in Dubai, United Arab Emirates.

— CHAPTER —
14

Follow Your Passion

Success isn't handed to us: we earn it.
—Misty Copeland

The phone rang, and I answered. The spokeswoman from secretary of state Hillary Clinton's office was calling to ask me if I was interested in serving on the Department of State's Council to Empower Women and Girls Through Sports. As a council member, I would travel to different parts of the world to share my story and encourage women and girls to pursue their potential through sports. By accepting the invitation, I would be joining an elite group of athletes, coaches, and sports journalists, like trailblazing legends Mia Hamm and Billie Jean King.

I was so shocked and humbled I didn't know what to say. I hadn't even qualified for the Olympics, but here I was being acknowledged for breaking barriers as the first Muslim woman to represent the United States in international competition. Having discovered my passion for international studies at Duke, I figured this would be an amazing opportunity to merge my interests in diplomacy with my love for sports. But was I up to this kind of challenge?

The State Department representative informed me that I could take a few days before I gave her an answer. So I used the time to talk to the people in my life I trusted most, beginning with my parents. I also talked to Peter and Keeth, and they—along with everyone else—were thrilled for me. So I accepted the position, my heart swelling with gratitude and pride.

One of the first assignments I had as a council member was a series of speaking engagements at local schools in London about my journey as a minority member of Team USA. I had a World Cup in London at the end of the week, so I flew in a few days before it.

While on the airplane, I went over my speech a dozen times. I was still getting the hang of speaking in front of large audiences, and this would be one of the biggest crowds yet. I wanted to make sure I was prepared because there was so much I wanted to say. I had to motivate these kids to follow their dreams no matter their gender, race, or religion. Most of all, I wanted them to know that I believed in them even if they didn't yet believe in themselves.

As it turned out, the first school I visited, the Sarah Bonnell School, had a large group of Muslim students. As students filed into the auditorium, girls wearing blue hijabs smiled when they saw me. I broke out in a huge grin and waved at them. Then I shared my experiences growing up in a town with few Muslims, speaking about how it was hard to be the only person with brown skin or the only person wearing hijab in the sport of fencing. I also shared with them that my secret to success was never to let other people's misconceptions about me stop me from pursuing my passions.

"When other people told me, 'No you can't,' that's when I told myself, 'Yes I can,'" I said. Looking out into the crowd of eager, cheerful faces, I was fulfilled. The rush of making a roomful of young girls feel good about themselves was amazing.

From that moment on, I made it a point to share my story as often as possible, not only through Secretary Clinton's initiative, but whenever the opportunity presented itself. I realized I was in a unique position to transform the way society saw Muslim women and black women in predominately white sports. I might also be able to change the way ethnic and religious minorities saw themselves. I wondered how my own journey might have been easier if there had been someone like me to look up to.

Soon, more and more speaking engagement opportunities came my way—at universities, Muslim conferences, and even some international events. The Muslim community gave me unconditional support, becoming like my extended family. I also think I cleared up a lot of the barriers Muslims had built against healthy living. While Islam doesn't restrict women from exercising, a lot of Muslim women find it difficult because most gyms are coed and workout wear is usually formfitting. It's become common for certain groups within the Muslim community, particularly South Asian and Arab families, to encourage their boys to be involved in sports, but not to do the same for their girls because of these issues. As a woman who pursued sport professionally in hijab, I proved that being a modest Muslim woman and being active were not mutually exclusive.

Another reason the Muslim community at large embraced me was because they were starved for positive representation in the media. Depictions of Muslims as radicals were all over our televisions and movie screens, fueling anti-Muslim discrimination. Then there was me: a Muslim American proudly playing for the country

I loved. The media thought I was a great story, though I found it fascinating that as anti-Muslim sentiment increased, the media's interest in me grew.

Of course, there would always be people, even Muslims, who didn't want to see me succeed. Some questioned things like my traveling without a *mahram*, or family escort, or criticized my uniform for being "too tight." But these were exceptions to the overwhelmingly positive responses I received from the majority of the Muslim community.

Everything seemed to be headed in the right direction in my life, and that included my faith. My new responsibilities changed and reshaped my conversations with Allah. Instead of praying for a win or praying during times of difficulties, I started to ask Allah to allow me to represent my community and my family well. I asked Allah to protect me from those who hated me and surround me instead with those who would encourage and uplift me. I asked Allah to help me show patience even when the world was testing me.

And, oh boy, was I tested.

Like a time I was traveling overseas for a series of training camps and competitions. My mom met me in Belgium for my last competition before heading home. As we were passing through a security checkpoint at the airport in Brussels, we were pulled out of line.

"You must take this off," the security officer said, pointing at my hijab.

I turned to my mother. She must have seen the fear in my eyes.

"What's the matter?" she asked.

"He's saying I have to take off my hijab."

Sensing the agent's negative energy, my mom calmly asked the security officer what the problem was. He repeated himself firmly, again indicating with hand gestures that we would have to remove our scarves.

"I'm sorry, we're wearing these for religious reasons. We're not taking them off," I said.

With the color in the officer's cheeks rising, he looked like I had insulted him personally.

"Off or no flight," he said. "You will not board the airplane if you do not take it off for the security check."

This had never happened to me before. My passport was now filled with stamps from dozens of different countries, and I had never been asked to remove my hijab at airport security.

"No. We're from the United States. We don't remove our hijab for security," I said. I knew this wasn't a necessary safety precaution. I was being profiled because of my religion.

"Take it off," the officer shouted, "or you will not fly on any airplane leaving this airport."

I looked around to see if anyone else had noticed our clear mistreatment by the security officer. It felt like a violation of my privacy to remove my hijab, like being asked to take off my own shirt. As redness rose in my cheeks, my mother spoke up. "Sir, how about you pat our heads down like this to check? That's how they do it in the United States."

"What is the problem here?" A female officer finally came over. The two officers spoke in hushed but heated tones in French, and then the female officer motioned for us to follow her. Mom and I exchanged looks and then followed the woman into a room not far from the security hall. Fearing that we were going to be questioned again, I reached for my mother's hand for comfort.

"Okay, ladies," the officer said. "Who is first?"

"For what?" I said.

"For the head check. I will pat you down over the scarf," the woman answered.

Before I could respond, my mother stepped forward. The whole procedure for both of us took five minutes, and then we were free to go. Relieved our ordeal was over, we thanked the woman and hightailed it out of there, eager to make our flight back home.

I didn't want to think what would have happened if my mother hadn't kept her cool. I was *not* going to remove my hijab; it was a violation of my religious rights to be forced to do so. But as I sat on the plane, I realized how important it was to stand up and fight against discrimination— no matter whom I was up against.

Sometimes I had to pinch myself when I thought about all the blessings, lessons, and self-awareness I'd gained because of fencing. I thought back to my darker days, when I was unemployed and hopeless, spending hours in front of the TV, and I felt thankful for every moment in my journey, including the obstacles, that had led me to this place where I could find happiness and purpose. Would I have been so lucky if I'd gotten a corporate job years before? Probably not.

But all the gifts did come at a cost. Between training, competing, and doing appearances, I was on the road so much that I felt exhausted half the time. Now and then I wondered if I would be able to make it through a single day. So when I was home, my favorite place to be was curled up in my bed or spending time with my family. I saw friends every now and then, but like I did during my time at Duke,

I chose to focus on fencing and training more than a social life. Luckily, my good friends understood my schedule, and they were happy to see me when I could hang out.

As if I didn't already have enough on my plate, though, in 2014—one year before the Olympic trials—I decided to start a business.

Any good business begins by solving a pressing need. In my case, I was having trouble finding modest, fashionable clothing—like long-sleeved maxi-dresses—to wear to my speaking engagements. Even when I was lucky enough to find them online, they were often from overseas, and that meant expensive shipping. One night when I was on the phone with my brother, Qareeb, who now lived in Los Angeles, I mentioned my frustrations.

"Why don't you make your own dresses?" Qareeb asked.

"I don't know how to sew," I said. I'd been online for an hour looking for a dress for an event, and absolutely nothing was right.

"No, silly," Qareeb said. "You should hire someone to make your dresses for you so you don't have to do this every time. In fact, you should start your own business making the types of dresses you're talking about. I'm sure there are plenty of Muslim women as frustrated as you. I know a manufacturer out here, actually."

My first thought was that my brother sounded crazy. Was it unrealistic for me to start my own clothing line while trying to qualify for the Olympics? I could barely find the time to sleep! But still, I opened my mouth and asked my brother, "So how would this all work?"

"Come up with some designs, and the next time you're out here I'll take you shopping for fabric. We can bring the sketches and fabrics to this manufacturer I know. She can make you some samples, and once you okay them, we can have them produced. You upload them to your website, and just like that, you'd be in business."

My brother made it sound so easy I started to think it might actually be possible to start a fashion company. "Okay, Qareeb, let me think about it," I said.

"All right," he said with a sigh. "I don't need to remind you that you can't fence forever. You gotta have a backup plan."

Once I hung up the phone, I stared at the clothes on my laptop screen. All the modest dress options were so dull and boring. I knew you could be fashionable *and* cover up, and I'd grown tired of spending time and money trying to do both. There had to be a solution for me—and all Muslim women—and I was going to find it.

Soon after that conversation with Qareeb, my sisters and I brainstormed ideas for the types of clothes we wanted to make. Full-length long-sleeved dresses.

Long-sleeved jumpsuits. Pants with tunic tops. Every modest option women needed to put together a stylish and versatile wardrobe. And we wanted all our pieces to be affordable, so being fashionable was accessible to all, not just the wealthy. Asiya and Faizah were just as excited as I was to launch this company, and soon this crazy idea Qareeb and I had cooked up became a full-on Muhammad family project. Even my mother got involved!

With Qareeb doing most of the legwork in Los Angeles to figure out the production side of things, my sisters and I focused on researching trends for design inspiration and finding the perfect web designer for our online site. Thanks to Qareeb's relationship with the manufacturer, there was a quick turnaround for our dress samples. Once we were able to hold the clothing samples in our hands, things felt real.

"This is really happening, you guys," I exclaimed to my sisters as we sat around our dining room table and looked over the dresses and tunics.

But before we could truly become small business owners, we needed investors. We decided my mom's sister, Aunt Diana, or Auntie as we liked to call her, would be the perfect person to pitch our business proposal to. Because Auntie and Uncle Bernard didn't have children of their own, they always said that helping us succeed made them feel like their money was being put to good use. But like my parents, Auntie spent her money only where she saw potential and passion. After she'd sat through a Power-Point presentation we put together, she was all in.

"What are you going to call the company?" she asked me when I finished pitching the idea to her.

"We were thinking about calling it Louella by Ibtihaj Muhammad," I said. "Louellashop.com for the website."

"You mean after your dad's mother?" she asked.

"Yeah," I said. "It's such a beautiful name, and I thought it would be a great way to remember her."

"That's really sweet," my aunt said with a smile. "You know family was the most important thing in the world to her."

"I know," I said, remembering how much I'd loved her.

Without hesitation, Auntie Diana said she would have a check ready for me the next day.

Louellashop.com was an instant success. Within the first year we expanded our offerings from ten items to more than fifty, and we made a profit. Our customers loved that our dresses were full length and came in a variety of colors, as well as the fact that most of our items were one hundred dollars or less *and* made in the United States. It was so much fun bringing Louella to life because I knew there was such a strong need for these clothes within the community. And not all our customers were Muslim! They came from different backgrounds and even different countries, but all had one thing in common—appreciation for modest fashion.

As someone who matched her hijab with her sneakers starting at a young age, I was thrilled to have this creative business venture that was helping other women look and feel good. Running a small business was a heavy load to take on, but when you've found your passion, it doesn't feel like work. I knew how to squeeze every minute out of a twenty-four-hour day, and after training, I would get on the train and update Louella's social media. At home I'd review sales and respond to customer e-mails. My sisters and my mother stayed busy managing orders and researching new design options for the next season. Everything about running an online clothing company was new to us, but we loved the challenge and the added perk of never being at a loss for what to wear. But perhaps the best part of starting Louella was that it gave me balance, something outside of fencing I could focus on. My thirtieth birthday was coming up, and I knew I had to have a life after fencing. For me, Louella might be it.

Dreams Can Come True

Be careful what you set your heart upon, for it will surely be yours.

—James Baldwin

By the beginning of 2015, I knew it was time for me to focus 100 percent of my energy on Olympic qualification. No sooner had Louella become a success than I had to abandon the day-to-day operations of the company and let my family handle the business full-time. I cut out all distractions from my life so I could focus only on fencing.

Unfortunately, despite our team's continued success in competitions, my teammates and coaching staff were still a problem for me. Our issues had become even bigger since a competition in Seoul, South Korea, earlier in the year. There, for the first time ever, I'd beaten Mariel.

The Seoul Grand Prix was the last competition before the Olympic qualifiers began. I had a tough bracket, but I advanced by knocking out some of the world's top fencers, including Ekaterina Dyachenko of Russia and Azza Besbes of Tunisia. But in the semifinals I had to face off against Mariel to determine who would fence for the gold against Ukraine's Olga Kharlan.

It was always a bit awkward to fence against my own teammate, but it was unavoidable. So when I put my mask on, my mind switched over to one thing: taking Mariel down. I realized it would be tough, but after being teammates with her for so long, I knew her strengths and weaknesses. Of course, that also meant she knew mine. Mariel and I had fenced countless times before, and in a lot of ways I was more prepared to fence her than anyone else I'd seen that day. Still, she was the most decorated US fencer in history, and I knew she wouldn't go down without a fight.

I said a prayer and stepped into it.

I scored the first point of the match, but after that I think she was out for blood. For the first quarter of our bout, Mariel stayed ahead of me by one or two points. But I fought back, and I could tell I was getting under her skin. She asked to stop to check the laces on her shoes, then repeatedly asked the referee to verify if the score posted on the machine was correct. It was apparent Mariel didn't believe I was able to keep up with her, or maybe she was just trying to throw me off.

It wasn't working. At the half I was ahead by a score of 8–7, and I think she started to get nervous. The lead kept going back and forth between us, and I once heard her mutter "Lucky" after I scored. She clearly didn't believe in my ability to beat her—but I believed in myself. I wanted that win more than anything. I wanted to show her that underestimating me was a mistake.

With Mariel leading 14–13, I parried her next attack and scored a point of my own. The score was now 14–14. Whoever got the next point would win.

At the start of the last point, I came out of the blocks fast, and Mariel used a false advance to get me to fall short in my lunge. Most fencers would have felt their back against the wall on defense, but this was where I was most comfortable. Mariel staged her attack, pushing me down the strip, and as she accelerated with her arm a little behind in speed, I was able to hit her.

Point for me! I won!

I advanced to the final, which guaranteed that I was going home with either a gold or a silver medal, my best finish ever at a grand prix. People in the audience clapped and cheered, and even the referee applauded my efforts.

But as I passed by Ed, he didn't even acknowledge me. Instead he ripped into Mariel.

"What were you doing out there?" he demanded. "How could you let her beat you?"

Mariel looked so hurt I almost felt sorry for her.

"She got lucky! They were all lucky touches!" she protested, still unwilling to admit that I was just a good fencer and had gotten the better of her that day.

I walked away. I wasn't going to let them steal this moment from me, but I knew a line in the sand had been drawn. It was clear I was seen as a threat, rather than an ally.

As if having to endure mistreatment from my teammates and coach weren't enough, I also had to deal with Akhi.

Akhi was still my coach, and unfortunately, he was still unreliable. But I loved what we'd built together, so rather than looking for a new coach, I started to take lessons with one of the foundation's other saber coaches, a man named Luke. Whenever I showed up to practice and Akhi wasn't there, Luke would immediately make time in his busy schedule for me. He and I never talked about Akhi; he just saw how hard I was working, and he must have felt sorry for me. Luke was pivotal in helping me maintain my precision and hand speed whenever Akhi wasn't there.

Akhi had given me so much in the years we'd worked together, and I owed much of my success to him. But I was disappointed by how disconnected we'd become. I needed someone wise to speak to, so I went to Peter often, knowing how much his heartfelt talks helped me. I wanted to be in the right head space as I approached the Olympic qualifying season. Without a dependable coach in my corner, and with the burden of unsupportive teammates to deal with, I needed some guidance.

"Hi, Peter," I said, knocking on his door. Peter was sitting in the coaches' room, glasses at the tip of his nose, his eyes buried in something. I'm sure my voice gave away my anxiety, because he immediately put aside his papers and told me to grab a seat.

"What's going on?" Peter asked gently.

I could feel my stomach in knots. There was a sense of doom hanging over me, and I knew it was going to ruin any chance I had of qualifying if I couldn't get my head in the right space.

"Peter," I started, trying to sound calm, but then the words just came tumbling out. "I know if I'm not top three in the nation at the end of the qualifying season, there's no chance they'll take me to the Olympics—"

"Ibtihaj," Peter interrupted me. "You're a God-fearing person, right? Well, whether you make the Olympic team or not has already been written by God. The team has no power in who qualifies or not. God has the power. The second you believe someone else does, you've defeated yourself."

"I know," I said, nodding.

"Fencing is an individual sport, Ibti, and you are the only one holding that saber on the strip. So don't look to anyone other than yourself for the success you want. You talk to God. You talk to me. And don't look to them for acknowledgment or empathy."

"That's it," I said, wanting desperately to have faith in Peter's words.

"Yep, that's it. If God wants this for you, then you will get it. Believe that and accept that."

I let Peter's words sink in, and I forced myself to acknowledge their truth. My religion had taught me to have faith in Allah. There is a saying in Islam, "What is meant for you will reach you even if it is beneath two mountains. What isn't meant for you won't reach you even if it is between your two lips." If Allah wanted me to succeed, no one—not the national coach nor my teammates—could change that.

I left Peter with the faith and confidence I needed. I told myself that whatever was meant for me would never miss me, and all I had to do was keep my head down and continue to grind. If it was meant for me to make the team, then Allah would give it to me. If not, that was Allah's will and I would accept it as such. So I let go of my anxiety and put my total faith in Allah. I was able to approach each competition from a place of faith, and I went on to have the most successful year of my life. I had more World Cup podium finishes and reached more finals than ever before, and I genuinely believe it was because I chose faith over fear.

In November we were about halfway through the Olympic qualifications in Paris, training at INSEP, the national French training center. I was practicing with one of France's top competitors, in the middle of an intense match, when I took a hard fall, severely spraining my right ankle. The pain was excruciating, and at first I thought my foot was broken. The team doctor hurried over to my side, helping me from the ground and over to the trainer's room. As the trainer assessed my injury, not one person from Team USA—fencers or coaching staff—came to see me.

The next morning I didn't go to practice because my ankle had swelled to the size of a softball. The team doctor instructed me to keep it elevated and compressed, and to ice it every few hours. I could barely walk, but that afternoon we had to leave Paris to go to the World Cup competition, which was being held in Orléans. I could barely maneuver with a crutch, but I had to keep up with the team, climbing up and down the Metro steps and through the cobblestone streets.

We finally made it to the train station, where we had to wait a few hours for our train to Orléans. I gratefully collapsed onto a bench, while Faizah sat next to me and tried to get me to prop up my ankle.

"I don't want you trying to be superwoman. If it hurts and you need to slow down, ask for help," she warned me.

I knew my sister was right, but I didn't want to be seen as weak. There were twelve fencers traveling altogether—the four from the national team and eight others who would also vie for a chance to go to the Olympics, including my sister—as well as the coaching staff and the team doctor. One of the fencers came over and announced that Ed was having an impromptu team meeting. I looked at Faizah, and without saying a word, she helped me to my feet. Together we walked to a nearby small café, where everyone was sitting around a few tables. Without any warning, Ed looked straight at me and said, "Ibtihaj, I don't understand why you weren't at practice this morning. Do you have an excuse for skipping?"

It took me a minute to register his words. The coach knew about my injury, so why was he calling me out as if I had done something wrong? As if I had a habit of skipping practices?

"Ed, I sprained my ankle. Remember, I couldn't even walk yesterday?" I said, trying against my better judgment to give him the benefit of the doubt. Was it possible he'd forgotten about my ankle, even though I was sitting there with my leg propped up?

Ed didn't say anything at first. Instead he stood there looking like he was trying to decide if he should believe me or not.

I stared daggers at him.

"Coach, she sprained her ankle," the doctor confirmed. "I taped it up yesterday, but it was pretty bad."

The coach looked down at my ankle, like he still needed some kind of verification.

"Well, you can walk now, so I don't believe that you're injured. You should have been at practice. Are you going to be able to compete tomorrow?" he asked.

Even though my ankle was throbbing, I pushed back my chair and stood up. "You've got to be kidding me! I don't need you to believe that I'm injured! Every one of you saw me fall yesterday. I can barely walk. I've never missed a practice. I've never led you to question my work ethic. You all don't even have the human decency to ask me if I'm okay!"

Faizah wrapped her arms around me and pulled me back down. I didn't know what had come over me, but I didn't care. I'd had it.

The next day I had to be ready for competition—no matter how bad I felt. So the team doctor taped my ankle as best he could, and I left the rest to Allah. I fenced on pure adrenaline and faith. I asked Allah before every match to help me through it. I don't even remember how I did it, but I won match after match and captured my first medal of the season that day. So if the coach and my teammates had counted me out of the Olympics running because of my injury, they were wrong.

After my ankle healed, I continued to do well throughout the season. My national ranking hovered between the number two and the number three spots, and the Olympic team now felt more like a possibility and less like just a dream. By early 2016 I knew I had a real chance before March—the end of the qualifying season—to make the team.

In February 2016 we were heading to a tournament in Athens, Greece. This was the second of two back-to-back competitions, and we had had a training camp in between, so I was traveling from Warsaw, Poland, following a weeklong camp. My mother, Faizah, and Akhi were flying directly from the United States to meet me in Greece, and I was so excited to see them.

The night before the competition was slated to begin, a sharp, grinding pain in my gut woke me up from a deep sleep. Instinctively, I jumped out of bed and raced to the bathroom. I barely made it there before I got sick. The waves of pain were so violent I couldn't even think—or make it back to bed. So I curled up on the bathroom floor, exhausted from the intensity of the sickness.

"Mom!" I cried out.

My mom pushed open the door to the bathroom. When she saw me, she ran for the phone and called the team doctor.

He came right away and immediately determined that I had food poisoning. Apparently, some of my teammates—all of whom had eaten food in the airport lounge—were suffering from the same symptoms, so I wasn't alone in my misery. Rather than prescribe anything to combat the illness, the doctor told me my body was doing its job and would rid itself of everything on its own. As I lay there on the bathroom floor, my face pressed against the cold blue and white tiles, I prayed to

Allah that I would survive the night. The pain was worse than anything I had ever experienced.

The next morning, while Faizah competed, I stayed back at the hotel. I still couldn't keep any food or liquids down, and my head was pounding. My muscles ached like I'd been run over by a bus, and whenever I tried to stand up, I was overcome with dizziness. I couldn't imagine trying to compete in this state, and luckily for me, because I was top sixteen in the world, I didn't have to until the second day of competition. Some of the other girls with food poisoning weren't so lucky, and somehow they had to find the energy to compete anyway. They didn't fare too well.

Unfortunately, neither did Faizah. I felt awful because I wasn't able to be by her side to support and coach her during this really important tournament. But there was nothing I could do.

The next day the team doctor gave me some medication that would at least allow me to keep water down and stop my head from pounding. I knew only a miracle would get me through a full day of competition, but it was moments like these that I'd trained for. I *had* to be ready.

When I walked into the arena in Athens, a sense of anticipation was in the air. Everyone was hoping to fence well enough to secure their spot at the Olympics. I knew I needed to warm up, but my body was too tired to do my normal routine, and I prayed it could function on auto-pilot. I repeated my mantras: *I'm ready. I'm prepared. I'm strong. I'm a champion.*

My energy was high in my first match, like I knew I had to get a jump on my opponent in order to stay in contention to win. And I did. I won that first match and went on to beat some tough fencers, including 2008 Olympic gold medalist Olga Zhovnir from Ukraine. Next in my bracket I had four-time Olympic medalist Olga Kharlan from Ukraine. I felt nervousness begin to creep into my system because Kharlan was such a formidable opponent. Before the match started, I took a moment for myself. I sat in the stands with headphones over my hijab, my eyes closed, and focused on my mantras and my breathing. Then Akhi gave me a quick pep talk, and when it was time to fence, I didn't have any extra energy to be nervous. I channeled everything into devising a game plan to fence Kharlan. It's amazing how during an episode of severe fatigue, your body remembers the countless hours of training and is able to push through. I beat Kharlan that day decisively by a score of 15–12, and I was so happy I almost collapsed into Akhi's arms when I hugged him.

My next match was in the semifinal round against Mariel. This time Mariel won. Even though I'd lost, I felt an overwhelming sense of happiness, relief, and pride that I was able to push through one of the most mentally and physically challenging days of my career. One of the benefits of being the athlete who is often overlooked is that it forces you to work harder, to keep your head down and grind out whatever task lies ahead. I ended the competition on the podium, thankful, and with the bronze medal around my neck.

After the medal ceremony I went to find my mother and Faizah in the stands. They were sitting near the rest of the American fencers.

"I'm so proud of you, Ibtihaj," my mother said as I sat down next to her. She hugged me tight, kissing my cheeks. I could tell she had been crying, not because she was sad, but because she was as excited as I was. She knew better than anyone the struggle of my journey. Since the very beginning, Mom had witnessed the roller coaster of emotions fencing had put me through, and it was a blessing to share this moment with her and Faizah.

My mom turned to Mariel and said, "Congratulations to you, Mariel. Great fencing."

Mariel didn't respond, only half turning to barely smile in our direction. Even her mother stayed silent. I was used to the cold treatment, but I couldn't believe that they would treat my mom, the most kindhearted person I knew, this way.

Back in our hotel room, I asked Mom, "Why do you

continue to congratulate them when they can't even respect you enough to say thank you?"

"It's not about them, Ibtihaj," Mom answered. "At the end of the day, I have to answer to Allah. That's it."

"But they're so mean! Even to you," I said, still fuming.

"Well, you have to show them that you're better than them. You always have to be kinder than them, and that's the way you hold up a mirror to their own dark reflections."

I shrugged. I found their immature behavior exhausting, but my mom was a good-natured, religious person, and that had always been the way she lived her life. She always tried to be a source of loving energy. It was a lesson I knew I needed to absorb more fully, because I wanted to be known as a good athlete *and* a good person.

Back home in Maplewood, I didn't dwell too much on my bronze medal because there were still a few qualifiers left, and I had to get to work to prepare for them. On Monday morning I sat down to plan my week, scheduling massage appointments, booking sessions with my trainer, and arranging lesson times with my coach. Afterward I was getting ready for the gym when I started getting text messages from friends and family congratulating me on qualifying for the Olympic team. It struck me as odd, but

I didn't pay the messages very much attention. I figured if I'd *really* made the Olympic team, I'd be the first to know.

As I brushed my hair into a tight ponytail and arranged my hijab, my phone beeped again, alerting me to another text message. Then came another, seconds later.

"Jeez," I said aloud, grabbing my phone and scrolling through the messages to see if there was anything important.

And there it was. A Google Alert flagging my name in an article posted on the US Olympic Committee website titled FENCER IBTIHAJ MUHAMMAD QUALIFIES FOR OLYMPICS, WILL BECOME FIRST US ATHLETE TO COMPETE IN A HIJAB.

I had officially qualified for the 2016 Olympic team! I screamed, "YES!" Then I tore out of my bedroom, dashed down two flights of steps, and found both of my parents on the couch in the living room.

"I qualified for the Olympic team!" I screeched, my phone still in my hand. I pulled the article onto the screen so they could read the news themselves. While they did, I did my own version of the happy dance. I bounced around the room in excitement. I jumped up in the air once, and then again, repeatedly screaming.

Mommy and Abu joined in my wild celebration,

hugging me and screaming with me. It felt surreal. I hadn't realized that by winning the bronze in Athens, I'd put myself so far ahead of my teammates that I qualified for the Games before anyone else. Now it was official, and no matter what happened in the last two months of the qualifying season, I was going to finish as either the number one or the number two ranked saber fencer in the United States. No one could take that away from me.

I was going to the Olympic Games to represent my country!

— CHAPTER —
16

Share Your Truth

The triumph can't be had without the struggle.

—Wilma Rudolph

Now that I'd made it onto the Olympic team, I had a chance to stop and really reflect. It had been almost ten years since I graduated from Duke, and it had been a long, hard road. I thought about the physical toll that getting to the Olympics had taken on my body, and then considered the emotional toll as well. Now that I'd realized the dream I'd held in my heart for years, had all the pain and suffering, of both my body and my mind, been worth it? Had it been worth knowingly putting myself through the most strenuous journey of my life?

Absolutely. I had *no* regrets. And now I could actually enjoy myself!

The first few days after I learned I'd qualified for the Olympics, I felt like I could finally exhale, like I'd been holding my breath for years. There was this huge sense of relief that I'd accomplished something most people could only dream of. But I didn't relax and soak it all in for too long; there was more hard work to come. In preparation for the world's most important sporting event, I knew I'd have to train even more.

Once you qualify for the Olympic team, staying healthy up until the day you compete at the Games is critical, so good nutrition and adequate rest are just as important as the days in the gym. Training becomes even more intense, and you take extra care to nurse every ailment. Additionally, the US Anti-Doping Agency holds random, mandatory drug tests for the top athletes in each sport. Athletes can be tested both in and out of competition. Every quarter you have to submit your locations over the next three months for possible drug testing. Officials can show up at practice, at home, or anywhere else to test you. If you miss the test or fail to submit your whereabouts for the quarter, you'll be disqualified from the Olympics.

Added to this pressure is the media. For most athletes who make an Olympic team, there's going to be some level of media attention. But I got more than most because of my hijab. As soon as Team USA put out a press release announcing me as the first US athlete in hijab to qualify for the Olympic Games, the phone didn't stop ringing.

I appreciated the media interest in my story, because our nation desperately needed to see that Muslims were just as American as anyone else. In fact, there had never been a more crucial moment for something or someone to change the perception of Muslims in America. During his presidential campaign, Donald Trump had publicly called for a ban on all Muslims entering the county, and by the late spring of 2016 he had suggested that the United States ban all immigrants from Muslim-majority countries. He'd even talked about creating a Muslim registry, which would force all Muslims to carry special IDs. I believe this kind of talk encouraged discrimination against Muslims and made it acceptable for people to commit violent acts against people like me. There'd been numerous cases of alleged hate crimes against the Muslim American community, mostly Muslim women who wore hijab, as well as physical and verbal attacks on the immigrant and LGBTQ communities, which had also been singled out by Trump.

I had a decision to make. As a US Olympian, would I stand on the front lines and publicly challenge this kind of hate?

I thought about one of my personal heroes, Muhammad

Ali, and his path to being an agent of change. Growing up, I knew Ali was one of the greatest boxing champions of all time. And as I got older, I came to know Ali for more than just his athleticism. I also came to know him for his activism against America's involvement in the Vietnam War, his efforts to fight racism with his words, and his devotion to humanitarian causes around the world. His public conversion to Islam in 1964 and his refusal to fight in the war threw Ali into the spotlight for his beliefs as a Muslim, not his boxing. Ali never caved to the pressure to reject Islam or fight in Vietnam, even with the threat of time in jail and a suspended boxing license. Muhammad Ali is the most famous and influential Muslim American of all time, and he taught me to stand up to those who try to divide us along the lines of religion. He showed us all what it means to have courage backed by religious belief. Muhammad Ali put the question of whether a person can be a Muslim and an American to rest, and his example encouraged me to stand my ground and share my truth.

I made a commitment to myself to seize every opportunity to unify people and challenge people's hateful, anti-Muslim beliefs, and I did dozens of interviews on TV and in the papers.

The *New York Times*, ESPN, ABC News, and *USA Today*, plus a few others, sent over production teams to interview me at the Peter Westbrook Foundation. But some media requests required me to travel to them instead. For example, one day I got an e-mail from *The Ellen DeGeneres Show*. They'd read about me in the press, loved my story, and wanted to pitch me for the show. I nearly dropped my phone in excitement as I read through the message. A few days later I Skyped with a producer, and I landed the gig.

Being on *The Ellen DeGeneres Show* was beyond a publicity opportunity. Ellen had one of the most popular television shows in the country and a massive global audience. She epitomized the attitude of being true to yourself, even when the costs are high, while simultaneously uniting people through love and laughter. Ellen was helping to make the world a little bit more tolerant and accepting. It was my hope that my appearance, as an unapologetic black Muslim woman in the sport of fencing who refused to give in to peer pressure, would help alleviate anti-Muslim sentiments. I imagined that seeing a Muslim American in hijab who wasn't on-screen to talk politics or terrorism, but rather something positive, like my Olympic journey, had to be a good thing.

I think it was. My interview with Ellen, as well as a fencing demonstration with one of her producers, was an experience I'll never forget.

The blessings continued. I appeared on *The Late Show with Stephen Colbert*, where I challenged him to a fencing match. At Team USA's 100 Days Out celebration in New York City, I taught First Lady Michelle Obama how to fence. In April, I was named one of *Time* magazine's one hundred most influential people in the world. I was featured in women's publications like *Glamour*, *Refinery29*, and *Allure*, where I was able to talk about why self-confidence is important both as an athlete and as a woman of color. I even got to meet with President Barack Obama a few times during his presidency.

I was often asked by the media if I thought my activism would stop big companies from wanting to work with me. To my surprise, a lot of them wanted to promote diversity and inclusion by endorsing athletes who looked or acted "different." So I partnered with companies like Visa, Nike, United Airlines, and Dick's Sporting Goods, whose ads pushed for social equality for all.

In many ways I felt like I proved all the haters in my life wrong. All the people who'd made me feel like I'd never succeed because of my race or my religion should be ashamed of themselves. I'd defied the odds. My success wasn't measured only by wins on the fencing strip, but also by the number of people I was able to inspire by sharing my story of triumph.

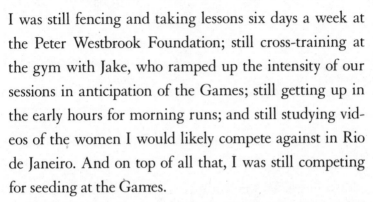

I was still fencing and taking lessons six days a week at the Peter Westbrook Foundation; still cross-training at the gym with Jake, who ramped up the intensity of our sessions in anticipation of the Games; still getting up in the early hours for morning runs; and still studying videos of the women I would likely compete against in Rio de Janeiro. And on top of all that, I was still competing for seeding at the Games.

My life had become a nonstop wild ride. But if I wanted to be truly prepared for the Olympics, that was just the way it had to be. You have to want to be successful more than you want to breathe. In the final weeks leading up to the Games, there were moments when the thought of my competitors training would wake me from my sleep before sunrise, forcing me out of bed to run, and sometimes I would feel so panicked just watching television that I would throw myself on the floor for a core workout.

Some days I would come to practice and the exhaustion would practically drip from my pores. A foil coach at the foundation, Buckie, saw me on one of these days and pulled me aside.

"If you're feeling really fatigued, you should go home," he said.

I tried to make a joke of it. "Do I look that bad?"

Buckie shrugged. "You look tired," he said firmly. "Go home."

"But I have to practice," I said emphatically.

Buckie shook his head. "Ibti, I've seen this a hundred times—training to the point of exhaustion day after day. You have to listen to your body. One day of rest isn't going to undo anything. In fact, your body will thank you for it later."

I could feel a knot in my throat. I didn't want Buckie to think I was weak. He was giving me permission to rest because I wouldn't allow myself, couldn't allow myself, to take a break. I started to say something more, but he turned to start his lesson. I realized Buckie was right.

That day I went home and took a nap. When I woke up, I took a slow walk around Maplewood and then helped my mother make dinner. The next day I felt so much better than the day before. Maybe setting aside a specific day for rest during the week wasn't such a bad idea.

Eventually I learned to incorporate recovery methods into my routine that would help reduce fatigue and bouts of exhaustion. I became very aware of my body and how I was feeling. If I strained a muscle during practice, for example, or felt fatigued after a long trip competing overseas, I wouldn't hesitate to take time off to give my body and mind a rest. I also started using acupuncture to treat old injuries, and weekly massages and ice baths to help prevent new ones.

Every night when I went to bed, my body and my mind were crazy with excitement and anticipation. It was the hardest season of my life, but I didn't regret a single moment of it. I knew it would be over far too soon, so I embraced the pain. I embraced the sacrifices. I embraced the opportunities, and I reminded myself along the way that every part of the journey was a blessing.

— CHAPTER —
17

Olympic Glory

If you stand for justice and equality, you have an obligation to find the biggest possible megaphone to let your feelings be known.

—John Carlos

Even though many people were concerned about Zika—a virus carried by mosquitoes that leads to birth defects, and which had infected thousands of people in Brazil—there was no way I was letting anything stand between me and traveling to the Olympics with Team USA. My parents never wavered on their promise to come to Brazil, and my family organized an online fund-raising campaign to help pay for everyone's travel and accommodations. Thanks to the financial support of my fans, eight members of my family—my parents, Asiya, Faizah and her husband, Qareeb and his wife, and my nephew, Zayd—traveled to Brazil to cheer me on in my quest for gold.

Every minute of my time during the Olympics was scheduled, from the moment I woke up in the morning in the Olympic Village until the blissful moment when I could lay my weary head down to rest at night. Both Ed and Akhi expected me and my teammates—Dagmara, Mariel, and a new teammate named Monica Aksamit— to train every day. The Games didn't officially start until August 5, following the opening ceremony, but we arrived on August 1 to get used to our temporary home. I was enchanted by Rio: the tropical warm air, the diverse faces of the locals, the bright pastel colors covering many of the buildings, the swaying palm trees on the streets. With its miles of sandy beaches, Rio felt like a grand tropical island instead of a major city in South America's largest country. But there was very little time to explore before competition started.

In addition to training at an off-site location twice a day, we had to sit for national and international media interviews. The dysfunction in the team had become almost normal, and I'm not sure anyone expected things ever to change. But when we sat for interviews, we acted like a team, and our first was on Copacabana Beach for the *Today* show the day after we arrived. From there the interviews kept rolling.

August 5 was the day of the opening ceremony. I finished a close second to Michael Phelps in the vote to determine who would carry the US flag. The flag bearer had been voted on by my US teammates across all sports, and I was honored even to have been in the running with world-famous athletes like Carmelo Anthony, Serena Williams, and Allyson Felix. I applauded Team USA because their decision to vote for a Muslim American woman in hijab was a powerful rebuke to the country's rising anti-Muslim sentiment. It was our collective act of resistance. In that moment my country's athletes came together and reassured me that they welcomed diversity and wanted to show the world what the United States truly stood for—inclusion.

The support didn't stop with the vote. As we marched into Rio's Maracanã Stadium that evening, I ended up walking in the front line only a few feet away from Michael Phelps and the American flag. Dressed in my white pants, navy-blue blazer, and white hijab, waving to the cheering crowds, knowing that more than three billion people were watching all over the world, I truly felt all parts of my identity were being applauded. The sense of pride I felt in that moment was off the charts.

My first day of competition was Monday, August 8. Unlike our World Cups, the individual event at the Olympics was held on one day. There were only thirty-two fencers competing in women's saber using a direct elimination format. Years of preparation and anticipation would come down to one day for individual events. Five days later, on August 13, we would have one day for the team competition. The warm-up hall was adjacent to the main competition hall, and it was small and cramped, with the thirty-two competitors, their coaches, officials, medical staff, and volunteers crowding the space. It was hard to find room to run and stretch, and even harder to find a quiet corner for my breathing and mantra ritual.

Before my first bout I went outside for a moment alone. As I stood under the warm Brazilian sun, I reminded myself to fence from a place of happiness and gratitude. Competing at the Olympic Games was a gift beyond my wildest dreams, and no matter what happened, I was proud of myself for making it this far.

Of course, I still wanted to win! On the world stage, I longed to taste Olympic glory more than I ever had in my life.

My first match was against a Ukrainian named Olena
Kravatska. We had fenced many times before, both in
individual and in team events, at World Cups and at world
championships. Any of the women from the Ukrainian
team would have been a tough draw, but Olena was about
six feet tall and a strong, relentless attacker. I'd already
consulted my notes to see what information I had com-
piled about her over the years from previous bouts, and I
saw that she used a lot of feints and depended on speed in
her attacks. I knew I would have to be patient and trust
my technique and instinct to win.

Before I stepped on the strip, I recited a quick prayer
and reminded myself to fight to the end.

Olena was a strong opponent, but I managed to stay in
the lead for the first few points. By the halfway mark she'd
surged ahead to lead by two, 9–7. I was so nervous that I
wasn't fencing my game. I was falling short in my attacks
and getting hit as I prepared for them. She was fast, and
I needed to slow her down. One of Olena's strengths was
her unwillingness to give up. I would score and take the
lead, and then she would follow up aggressively, winning
a point. Back and forth we went, exchanging the lead.
Her primal screams, which sounded like an angry moun-
tain lion's, would ring throughout the stadium and then
be answered by my own screams of triumph.

We were deadlocked, 13–13, and I needed only a few more points to be declared the winner and move on. When the referee said, "Fence," Olena flew from the on-guard line, launching a long attack. I made two advances to close the distance, and I matched each of Olena's advances with a retreat. I kept my blade out in front of me and could sense that Olena was holding back a bit. I unexpectedly shifted my weight to my front foot and hit her on her right arm. Olena couldn't block my blade, and she slipped and fell to the ground. The point was mine! I now led 14–13 and needed to score only once more.

But there was no time to think. I was back at the on-guard line, saber raised. The sounds of the cheering crowd, the sweat rolling down my back and pooling in my armpits, the smell of my own breath filling my nostrils behind my mask, all meant nothing. I shut everything down except the instinct to score. I waited for the signal to begin. Olena came at me, and just as before, I used the same action to score, and Olena was unable to get her light on.

I did it! I DID IT! I couldn't contain my joy. I raised my arms in triumph and did a quick lap around the strip. I pulled my mask off and shrieked. The only sound louder than my screams at that moment were my brother Qareeb's shouts from the stands. He was so excited for me that he had everyone in the stands cheering, "USA! USA!" I turned around and saw my whole family on their feet, fists pumping, hugging one another and shouting my name. I ran over to them and just let their happiness wash over me. I could not believe I was now going to the table of sixteen.

"Ibtihaj, you can do this," Faizah said, practically screaming down to me, hoping her words reached me over all the stadium noise. "You can really do this!"

I squeezed her hand and tried to convey how much I loved her and appreciated her. I knew that if it weren't for Faizah working with me, supporting me, and keeping me sane, I wouldn't be in Rio. This win was just as much Faizah's as it was mine. I was so emotional I could feel myself start to cry. I owed everything to my family and their undying support for me. My parents had worked so hard to support my fencing career since I was twelve years old, and my siblings never complained about all the time, resources, and attention my fencing had required of the family. With each of them in my corner, I felt like anything was possible—even bringing home a medal from the Olympic Games.

"Are you ready for your next bout?" Qareeb asked me. "I want to see you tear the next girl apart just like you did this one. You were amazing out there."

Before I could respond to my brother, we were interrupted by a volunteer who insisted I had to leave the fencing floor. As I walked back to the warm-up hall, there was a throng of reporters who were clamoring to get a comment from me following my first win. At the Olympics there isn't a lot of time between bouts, and I needed every single minute to prepare for my next match. I turned to the pack of reporters, saying, "Sorry, I have to go prepare." Then I ran off to strategize.

I was fencing a woman from France named Cécilia Berder in my next match. I'd beaten Cécilia the last few times we'd met, but she was very good. In fact, she was the best saber fencer in France at the time and ranked ninth in the world, right behind me.

I didn't go into the bout overconfident because I knew she'd be a tough opponent. So as I stepped out on the strip, game face on and ready for battle, I tried to calm my mind. Right before the bout started, I recited a quick prayer. I remembered the look of pride and hope on Faizah's face, and her words ran through my mind. *You can really do this!* Yes, I could.

I walked out onto the strip to the sounds of the fans cheering, "USA! USA!" But I tuned it all out and focused on my opponent. I came out on fire, quickly jumped to a 6–2 lead, and started to taste victory. But Cécilia rallied hard. She scored a few points, tying us up, and then we traded turns taking the lead. I was having trouble focusing, though, frequently getting distracted by the noise of the crowd. I knew how much they wanted me to win.

When I heard the signal to fence, I exploded out of the box and landed a point on Cécilia right away, barely leaving her time to parry. The match stopped, but the referee didn't call a point for me. I knew I'd landed that touch, and I asked the ref to look at it again on his screen. But he still refused to give me the point.

I couldn't believe it. I threw my mask to the ground in anger and cried, "What?!" I knew it was bad form to argue with the ref's call, but I was sure I'd scored that point. Instead of agreeing with me, the ref gave me a yellow card, warning me for false-starting. I was so mad, but I had to try to get myself under control. To refocus and get back into the match. So I put my mask on and used my anger to push harder.

Cécilia and I traded points, but I couldn't seem to find my groove. When the score was 12–14 in her favor, I knew I didn't have any room for error. I thought I was ready, but after falling short in my attack, Cécilia took over, patiently staging her moment as she moved down the strip. We soon neared the end of my side of the strip, and my foot slipped. I ended in an awkward split with one foot out of bounds, losing the point. Cécilia won the match, 15–12.

It was over. I had lost, ending my individual competition.

I was devastated and furious at myself, and I could feel tears welling up before I took off my mask. I felt like I'd let everyone down. *I shouldn't have lost*, I kept thinking. *How did I lose?* As shame overwhelmed me, I peeled myself off the ground, shook hands with Cécilia, and walked off the strip. My dreams of an individual Olympic medal were over.

I dodged the reporters shouting questions and found a place with Faizah to lick my wounds. Then I sobbed for more than half an hour. No matter how much you tell yourself you're just happy to make the team, losing is incredibly painful—especially to someone you know you're capable of beating. I kept replaying each point in my mind and thinking what actions I could have done differently, and then, as I thought about all the people who'd been cheering for me, I started to cry even harder.

Thankfully, my family members were there to offer words of encouragement and support. My mom reminded me that just competing in the Olympics was a win for me and for all the people who looked up to me. I was an example for them, and even though I hadn't finished as well as I had hoped—the individual competition ended with me in twelfth place—I was one of the best female saber fencers in the world. I should be proud of that.

My father was the last person to speak after my loss. Wiping away my tears, he said, "Ibtihaj, it's okay. You win some. You lose some. But you gave it everything you had today."

"But I lost my second match," I whispered.

"Ibtihaj, I've never seen anyone work as a hard as you do, especially out there today. In my eyes, you won that gold medal today."

"Thanks, Abu," I said, warming at my father's words. I knew Abu wasn't the type to say things just to make me feel better. He meant it, and that was everything to me.

It took me about an hour to compose myself. I knew the press was waiting for a statement from me, and I didn't want to come out tearstained and sniffling. So I tried to get in touch with my rational self. I knew that I'd absolutely done my best, and I searched inside my soul and knew I had no regrets. Losing on the world stage stung, but in time the pain would fade, and I was going to be okay.

When I went out to meet the press, I tried to present a picture of resolve and acceptance. As I stood in front of the sea of cameras and microphones, someone spoke up.

"How do you feel about losing to Cécilia Berder?"

I pulled in a deep breath and responded. "Cécilia is a great competitor, and she bested me today. Win or lose, competing here today was bigger than any of my own personal ambitions."

The next question came as soon as I finished my last words.

"How do you feel as a Muslim woman competing in these Olympics, considering what's going on in your country?"

This was a critical moment for me. I knew my answer would get a ton of coverage, so I was succinct. "I think that anyone who has paid attention to the news would know the importance of having a Muslim woman on Team USA at this moment of time. In light of all the political fuss that's going on, I think my presence on the team challenges those misconceptions that people have about who a Muslim woman is and can be."

The questions continued for close to an hour. Through it all I tried my best to represent my country and my family with honor and dignity.

As it turned out, no one from the US women's saber team did well in the individual competition. Dagmara lost her first match, and Mariel lost in the second round, just as I had. So the three of us were motivated to reclaim our glory during the team competition five days later.

As a team, we were underdogs. Though we had medaled in the world championships for the last five years, taking home the gold in 2014, we hadn't been able to secure even one medal at any of the World Cups this season. Together we'd had so many injuries and had struggled to find our rhythm, so we weren't going in overconfident.

The team competition on August 13 arrived after four days of grueling practices with Ed. Now that I knew exactly what to expect at an Olympic competition, I felt more confident than I had before my individual matches. It was also easier knowing that I had my team to support me on the strip. I still don't know how we did it, but somehow that day everyone pushed aside the personal feelings that had defined our squad for the last several years. Maybe we were all too disappointed by how we'd performed in the individual competition, or maybe our thirst for Olympic glory was bigger than anything else in the world. Regardless, we put aside the chaos and went out there as a team.

The first team to reach forty-five points would win. Our first match was against Poland, and I knew they'd fight to the very end. We almost let an eleven-point lead slide through our fingers, but in a valiant last-bout effort Mariel pulled us back for the win.

In the semifinal round we faced the formidable Russian team. I knew they would be our toughest opponents of the day—not just because the fencers were great, but also because the referees seemed to love them. We hung in there most of the match but had a large deficit going into the seventh bout. Luckily, I was on fire when I went up against Ekaterina Dyachenko. I outscored her 13–4, giving us a narrow one-point lead, 35–34.

Unfortunately, we couldn't hold on to the lead, with Dagmara failing to score any points in the eighth match. In the end the margin was too large for Mariel against world number two Yana Egorian, and the Russians beat us.

The Olympics weren't over for us, though. We had one more chance for glory.

Because we'd lost in the semifinals, we'd be fencing in the bronze-medal match—this time against Italy. As we walked into the call room to have our equipment checked prior to the start, I could tell something was off about their team. They looked defeated. Sure, we'd both just lost, but the Italian team looked like they were struggling to move past it. We knew there was no time to sulk, so we were ready.

Dagmara was the first one on the strip, and Mariel, Monica, and I stood on the sidelines to cheer her on. The match started out well, with Dagmara looking strong and decisive, and she ended up winning 5–2. From then on, each of us took turns defending and maintaining USA's lead. When Mariel scored the final winning touch, securing our forty-fifth point, we knew we'd done it. The three of us ran onto the raised strip and wrapped Mariel in grateful hugs. No one had given up, no one had failed. The final score was 45–30, and I was *so* happy. We had triumphed as a team. Everyone had done what they had to do, and we had prevailed—despite our differences. I had never felt so proud. There on the strip we hugged, high-fived, and basked in our glory. For a moment I forgot about everything except the win. Every single sacrifice felt worth it in that beautiful moment. Every injury, every tear, every snub by my teammates—it all washed away as we reveled in the sound of the crowd cheering us on.

Later that day during the medal ceremony, every single one of those feelings of gratitude and awe was magnified. I was so proud to stand under the Stars and Stripes in that arena. And even though I'd watched countless Olympic Games on television, and sometimes even teared up during a particularly emotional medal ceremony, there was nothing that could have prepared me for the feelings that swept over me when they announced the United States as the bronze medalist. At the sound of our country's name, my teammates and I clasped hands and held them high in triumph as we stepped up onto the podium together. Then one by one our names were announced, and our medals were carefully placed over our heads. I felt a burst of pure, unadulterated joy, pride, and awe. As an athlete, I had the ultimate prize hanging around my neck: an Olympic medal. Despite the obstacles and the never-ending chorus of naysayers, I had accomplished what I set out to do with my saber, and it was the sweetest feeling of satisfaction I'd ever had.

After the Olympic Games, I was physically and mentally exhausted. The day after I got home, I dropped my bags in my room, then got in a car with my sisters and my niece and drove south to spend the week with my parents at the beach in Ocean City, Maryland. While everyone spent the day frolicking in the sand and water, I stayed in the hotel room so I could soak in the silence. As much as I loved my family and was grateful to spend time with them, I needed to be alone.

Thankfully, my family understood, and they encouraged me to take as much time as I needed to relax and decompress. So I did. For almost an entire week I lay in bed, only occasionally joining my family for dinner or a walk on the beach. I tried not to think about fencing, training, or what would come next. I just let my mind wander and rest.

Of course, my self-imposed vacation from life couldn't last forever. I had previously booked speaking engagements and appearances, plus I had other responsibilities, like Louella. Our online store was still growing, and my sisters needed me to be more than the face of the company. Just two weeks after the Olympics, I went with my family to Chicago for the largest Islamic conference in North America, where I networked and talked up our brand in our Louella booths. But I barely had a moment to feel happy about this wonderful business I'd help build before I had to deal with a more pressing issue.

Someone wanted me dead.

The e-mail had come through USA Fencing. Some disgruntled American referred to me as "a thing that had to be destroyed." He threatened to kill me and my family, and threatened USA Fencing for having me on the team. It was the scariest thing I'd ever read. I'd never considered myself ignorant of the hate that existed in the world, but I was terrified—not just for me, but for my family as well.

What was I to do in a situation like this? Luckily,

USA Fencing officials and my management team took the matter seriously right away, and they approached law enforcement.

Because the man had made actual death threats against me and my family—threats that could be considered hate crimes—the FBI got involved. Investigators traveled to the man's home in Virginia, and it was eventually determined that he didn't pose a "real threat." He supposedly was just "blowing off some steam online." While I was grateful that the authorities had taken such quick and decisive action, this death threat only confirmed what I had feared all along: that as my visibility rose, hateful people would make every effort to hurt me and my family. My social media pages were already full of unsavory comments from people who had a problem with everything about me, from my hijab to my taste in movies. Up until this point I had been able to brush off that negativity as mere Internet nonsense, but this latest threat made it all too real.

I had to ask myself, *Is it all worth it?* As the nation became more racially and politically polarized, did I really want to take a stand at the risk of my own safety? One day I'd feel brave and resolute to keep speaking up even in the face of danger, but the next day I'd wonder how I would ever be able to go out into the world as a symbol of courage when I actually felt fear.

Both my mom and my dad were extremely shaken by the death threat, even though it had amounted to nothing. As a retired police officer, my dad wasn't convinced that the threat was truly over, and he blamed himself for not being able to protect me.

"You see, Ibtihaj," Abu said, "this is why sometimes it's just good practice to say nothing and let your actions speak for you. You've been a positive symbol for so many people, but maybe it's time for you to pull back from all the speeches and the media interviews. That just gives these guys more to use against you."

I didn't know what to say. My father was right: My increased visibility brought new opportunities, both good and bad. But if I went silent, I'd be letting the crazies win.

"But this isn't a game, Ibtihaj," he said. "This is your life we're talking about here."

I sighed. There was a lot of truth in what my dad was saying. His first concern—like it had always been—was his family's safety.

"But, Abu, I've been given this opportunity. If I don't speak up, who will?"

"I don't know, Ibtihaj," Abu admitted. "But I can't let anything happen to you."

My dad would never have forced me to quit speaking out, but he also wanted to make sure I took the right precautions. For one, he wanted me always to travel with some kind of security team.

"You want me to walk around with bodyguards, Abu?" I said, laughing as I imagined myself flanked by six burly men in dark suits and sunglasses at my next speaking event.

Abu wasn't laughing. "Yes, I do. And I know people who can provide the services."

On September 10, 2016, the city of Maplewood celebrated Ibtihaj Muhammad Day with activities and a parade. The event had been planned since before the Olympics, and my bringing home a bronze medal only made the organizers more excited to celebrate. I was flattered by the idea, but the recent events with the FBI, and my father's warnings, had me a little skittish about walking through Maplewood with crowds of people around me. Even though it was home, I was still concerned about my safety.

My parents were, too, and they asked the city to offer protection. I was glad they did. The city police were terrific and made me feel as safe as possible. And the whole day turned out to be a life-affirming experience, making me feel like I really *was* inspiring and helping others.

I couldn't believe the number of people who came out to celebrate. The streets were packed with pedestrians holding signs and banners that said things like GO IBTIHAJ MUHAMMAD! and HOMETOWN HERO! People were yelling and cheering as I passed by in a convertible.

"We love you, Ibtihaj," I heard more times than I could keep count.

When we got to the steps of the Maplewood library, I received a handful of official awards and proclamations from various city officials, as well as artwork and letters from local artists. It was so humbling—especially the fact that it wasn't just Muslim people or black people who came out. Here I had the diverse citizens of an entire city singing my praises, congratulating me on my achievements, and that made me really think about the power of my story. I had the opportunity to touch people's lives and to make a difference in the world. I wasn't going to let the hateful words of anyone define my life or change my journey. I wasn't going to live in fear. I refused to silence my voice when I knew I had the potential to change the world. Indeed, Allah had a plan for me, and I was going to keep riding this ride to see how far it could take me.

— EPILOGUE —

I decided to keep fencing. I had accomplished my goal of going to the Olympics, but I couldn't stomach the thought of retiring. I was still ranked number two in the country and number twelve in the world after the Olympics. And despite the fact that Louella was experiencing consistent growth, and I was being asked to speak on panels and at conferences all over the world, I still felt like a fencer through and through.

My professional network and my opportunity to be an agent for change had truly blossomed. Alongside four other well-known athletes—NFL player Michael Bennett, WNBA stars Brittney Griner and Breanna Stewart, and track-and-field legend John Carlos—I helped create a nonprofit organization called Athletes for Impact, whose mission is to "connect athletes with communities to positively transform America." Through it, we address issues from climate change to mass incarceration. With sports figures dominating headlines for using their voices to speak on matters they believe in, we realized that, if unified and organized, athletes can have a huge impact on the world, not just on the field.

I'm not sure what I would even put on a traditional business card: "Olympic fencer"? "Activist"? "Entrepreneur"? All of the above? But I eventually came to understand that it's about embracing the flexibility and possibility of the unknown. That I can define my identity and that I don't need to explain myself to others or have them define me.

One of the most exciting things that happened to me after the Olympics was that the Mattel toy company decided to make an Ibtihaj Muhammad Barbie doll. She would come dressed in a fencing uniform with a hijab! As I sat in the conference room at Mattel, my mascara running from my tears as I looked at the prototype, I tried to explain why this doll was going to be so important to so many little girls.

What's more important than what my doll looks like is what my doll stands for—reminding kids everywhere that they can be anything.

Black, white, Muslim, Christian, Jewish, boy, girl... anyone. Don't ever give up on your dreams. Work for them. Embrace them. They make you who you are.

— ACKNOWLEDGMENTS —

All praises to the Most High, the Most Beneficent, the Most Merciful. I thank Allah for giving me this beautiful life, the experiences of joy, of sadness, and everything in between. *Alhamdulillah.*

To my mother and father, thank you for seeing potential in me even when I had a hard time seeing it in myself. Your efforts to instill values like hard work and dedication have shaped me into who I am today. You taught me the importance of sacrifice, preparation, and responsibility. It is through you I learned to have an unwavering love for Allah, His plan, and my faith. It is my hope that I will continue to make you proud and that your love and guidance helps me in every step along my journey.

To my sister Faizah, thank you for always being the calm in every storm and the wind beneath my wings. Though we are six years apart, I like to think of us as twins, coupled on this adventure into the world of elite fencing. We trained together every day, helped each other through the moments that mattered most, and never stopped rooting for each other's personal success. This Olympic medal is as much Faizah's as it is my own. Here's to always being best friends.

To my brother Qareeb, sisters Brandilyn and Asiya, and Auntie, I am forever grateful for the endless support and love. To my niece Maliha and nephew Zayd, because of you I strive to leave the world a better place.

To my personal coaches, Akhi, Frank, and Alex; trainer Osei; and the other coaches who helped me along the way, Achiko and Zoran; thank you for preparing me physically, tactically, and mentally to become the best version of myself.

To Peter Westbrook, thank you for paving the way for black and brown kids everywhere and for making this dream a possibility for me. To my Foundation teammates and mentors, friends Isis and Paola, thank you for your unconditional love and support. What a blessing it is to have family by your side during your wins. What an even greater blessing it is to have family by your side during your falls.

To Joel Hirschhorn and Andrea Buccino, thank you for putting the pieces back together again.

To Lindsay and Mary, I will be forever grateful for

your guidance and friendship and for encouraging me to awaken my inner activist.

I want to thank Greg for showing me the importance of deadlines and guiding me through the book-writing process. Big thank you to Lisa and the team at Little, Brown.

One last thanks to Sarah Durand. Your help on this project was instrumental, and your care for my memoir made it a story I'm proud to share with young readers everywhere.

— GLOSSARY OF FENCING TERMS —

advance: One of the basic footwork techniques in fencing. With the feet perpendicular to each other and spaced apart, the fencer pushes off with the rear foot, lifts the toes of the front foot, and then pushes forward with the rear foot, moving the entire body forward.

attack: The act of pushing forward toward the opponent in an attempt to score a point.

body cord: The insulated wire that connects the fencer's vest, or lamé, to a scoring machine. When the lamé is touched by the sword, an electric current runs through the body cord to the machine, registering a point.

bout: A competition between two fencers in which the score is kept. A synonym for *match*.

épée: One of the three types of swords used in fencing. The body of an épée is heavier than a foil or saber, and it is three-sided, or triangular. When one fences épée, the opponent's entire body is the target area, and points can be scored only if the tip of the blade touches the opponent.

false attack: An attack in which the sword intentionally falls short of touching the opponent or misses them entirely. Like a feint, it's intended to trick an opponent.

false start: A situation in which one fencer tries to attack before the referee calls "fence," signaling that the bout should begin.

feint: A sword movement designed to fool or distract an opponent, making them think the attacker will do one thing when, in fact, they do another.

foil: One of the three types of swords used in fencing. The body of a foil is rectangular and very light (less than one pound). When one fences foil, the torso and the groin comprise the target area, and points can be scored only if the tip of the blade touches the opponent.

grip: The part of the sword that the fencer holds during a bout.

lamé: The electrically conductive vest worn over a fencer's jacket, to which a body cord is connected.

lunge: An offensive footwork technique in which a fencer kicks forward with the front foot, pushes forward with the back foot, and enters a wide-legged, often squatting position.

match: A competition between two fencers in which the score is kept. A synonym for *bout*.

parry: A defensive move in which the blade blocks an opponent from making a point.

referee: The official who scores, determines penalties, and ensures the safe execution of a match.

retreat: One of fencing's basic footwork techniques, which is the opposite of the advance. The fencer pushes off with the front foot, then lifts the back foot, moving the body backward.

saber: One of the three types of swords used in fencing. The body of a saber is I or V shaped, and the tip is blunted. When one fences saber, everything from the waist up, including the head but excluding the hands, comprises the target area, and points can be scored if the tip or the side of the sword touches the opponent.

strip: Also called the *piste*, this is the legal playing area in fencing. If a fencer steps out of the strip, a point is awarded to their opponent.

target area: The area of a fencer's body that, when touched by an opponent's sword, registers a point.

— IBTIHAJ'S ADVICE —

Hold on to your faith first and foremost.

Be open and receptive to advice and suggestions
from those who have experience.

Believe that whatever is meant for you
will never miss you.

Dream big, and trust that with a lot of hard work,
anything is possible.

Don't be afraid to ask for help.

Find a sport or activity that makes you happy.

Respect your teammates' level of competitiveness and
ability. Not everyone is at the same level.

Write down your strengths and things you want
to improve. With time and dedication,
you'll see results.

It's not always about the win. Progress is also winning.

Be your own cheerleader. Always feed yourself
motivational and encouraging words.

Find balance. Rest and recovery are just as important as training itself.

Always seek knowledge in whatever you do. Do your research, take notes, and be willing to learn.

Don't be afraid to pat yourself on the back. Love and appreciation of self is vital. You've worked hard!

Be open to people who may be different from you. Tolerance and acceptance of differences make for improved, more inclusive, richer spaces.

We all have a gift that we can use to make the world a better place. What's yours?

— Q&A WITH IBTIHAJ —

Q: In *Proud*, you talk about the challenges of growing up feeling different, and of being treated differently because of who you are. If you could go back in time, what would you tell your younger self?

A: I would tell myself to be brave and never fear speaking up. I used to get in trouble for being opinionated and outspoken, oftentimes being made to feel as if they were flawed traits. I've learned to embrace my outspokenness and use my voice for things that are important to me, like the fight for social justice.

Q: You've already accomplished so much, and have a busy schedule with your own business, athletic training, and endorsement deals. What made you decide to write a book?

A: It was important for me to share my story of resilience. I want young readers to know that the journey may not be easy, but their dreams are never out of reach. The impossible is possible.

Q: It's clear in *Proud* that you're extremely close to your family. Did you have any memorable moments with them, going through photos or sharing memories as you wrote the book?

A: Going through family photos with everyone was a lot of fun. My parents shared a lot of memories and funny stories. I have a niece (Maliha, two) and nephew (Zayd, nine) with whom I get to spend a lot of time, and it was mind-blowing to see myself at their age through photos.

Q: What does it mean to you to know that your book, featuring a powerful, proud African American Muslim woman in hijab on the cover, is available on school, library, and bookstore shelves across the country?

A: It is humbling to know we are at a time in our country when we can celebrate one another for our differences. I embraced what made me stand out and shattered stereotypes in the process. I hope to encourage young girls and boys, Muslim and non-Muslim, to do the same.

IBTIHAJ MUHAMMAD

is a fencer and the first Muslim American woman in hijab to compete for the United States in the Olympic Games. She is also the first female Muslim American to medal at the Olympic Games, winning bronze in the women's saber team event. Named one of *Time* magazine's 100 Most Influential People in the world, she serves as a sports ambassador for the US State Department, cofounded Athletes for Impact and her clothing company Louella, and inspired the first hijabi Barbie in her likeness.

Ibtihaj invites you to visit her online at

ibtihajmuhammad.com

⊙ ibtihajmuhammad   🐦 @ibtihajmuhammad

🅕 @ibtihajmuhammadusa